STRUCTURE
The Master Key to KINGDOM SUCCESS

STRUCTURE
The Master Key to KINGDOM SUCCESS

DR. FINACE BUSH

Unless otherwise noted, Scripture quotations are taken from the KING JAMES VERSION (KJV) of the Holy Bible. Amplified quotations are indicated as (AMP). New Living Translation quotations are indicated as (NLT). All versions used by permission of the copyright owners.

Published in Georgia by:

Dr. Finace Bush
P.O. Box 7690 N
Augusta, S.C. 29861
Web address: www.FBJM.org
Email: f.BushPublishing@fbjm.org

In conjunction with Carsamonte Publishing
www.carsamonte.com

Editorial and publishing assistance provided by:

Carmen Santos Monteiro, ghostwriter, editor, and author of **"Blood Stains:** *All in the Name of Love," "Side Gig," and "Cre`me and Sugar at Midnight"* (query@carsamonte.com / www.carsamonte.com).

First-line editing to a portion of this book provided by: Mignon Spencer.

Cover and interior Design by:

Cassandra West of Whole Armor Design (www.wholearmordesign.com / cwest@ wholearmordesign.com)

Structure: The Master Key to Kingdom Success was printed in the United States of America.

ISBN 978-0-9830614-4-1

Dedication and Acknowledgments

I dedicate this book to my lovely wife, Denise, who stands by my side and is truly a gifted helpmate and assistant. To my four special children working with us in ministry: Cattina, Teaya, Finace III, and Augustus. To my special grandchildren: Finace J. IV, Finace J. V, Jada, Joshua, and Jaden. To my two sons-in-law who consider themselves my paternal sons and to my numerous spiritual sons and daughters; I dedicate this work to you.

A special thanks to the Crown Christian Church International family; local and abroad; to my covenant brothers and partners who share in this great mission to plant, establish, and expand the Kingdom of God. To my special friends and members who assisted with typing, copying, and a variety of other ways to prepare for publishing. A special thanks to the plethora of traditional, contemporary, and classical writers, along with the Holy Spirit, who shaped my beliefs and convictions over the last forty years. To the most dedicated, supporting, and loving parents for whom a young man could ask: My most consistent prayer was that God would allow me to complete a project that the two of you could be proud of because your sacrifices are limitless. You deserve a crown for a job well done in rearing your four children; I will love and honor you always.

To Rhonda, Harold [Fat's] and Cheryl, may God continue to bless and prosper each of you. To my special teachers and mentors; Apostle Frederick K. C. Price, D.D., Dr. Myles Munroe, William Evans, Kenneth Hagin, and OG Mandino. To my dedicated and most admired spiritual coverings Dr. Creflo and Taffi Dollar. You provoke, inspire, and motivate me to strive for excellence in all I do. Your spiritual ambitions and Kingdom agenda for spreading the Gospel over the world challenges me to do likewise. Thanks for your many feats of inspirations. I extend my highest honor and most sincere thanks to my Father God, His Son, Jesus (my elder brother), and His precious Holy Spirit. You are responsible for inspiring this work through me. I thank you eternally.

FOREWORD

STRUCTURE; the very title commands attention. My first question about this subject was what could possibly be stated in a two-book series? Initially, I thought it is such a broad subject and I wondered how it could ever be narrowed into a two-book series. I thought for sure such a broad subject would be all over the place. Well, the structure Dr. Bush presents throughout the pages of this series is not only action-provoking but it promotes realistic assessments that can build structure and order in the life of every reader. Dr. Bush poignantly addresses all areas of human existence: Vision, time, relationships, money, faith, confessions, thoughts, and emotions. All of these areas require structure in order to master. .

Much like he provides to his congregation when providing tools for successful living, Dr. Bush has both lived and shares the steps to master structure in his own life. He lived it and he is thusly able to provide real-life, hands-on confirmation to the complexities and challenges in the two-book series. During his previous twenty years of life these well-defined lines of structure were being methodically and supernaturally created, where each "T" was crossed and every "I" dotted in a blueprint that navigates readers to mastering behaviors that are proven to yield a successful life.

When Dr. Bush first approached me about editing his book, I was honored to be chosen for such an anointed project. I was excited and knew that he would thoroughly cover the intricate points of his topic or any other. Little did I know the treat I was in for ... that this project would play a pivotal role in my own life. I never expected that it would be a challenge to remain focused on editing these pages; but it was. I would actually stop, take notes, and work the various exercises because it ministered so much to my own life.

Right away, I identified a lack of structure in my own time management. I discovered that I was not effectively assigning my time. Time is a precious resource that once wasted, it can never be regained. Not to say that other opportunities would never present themselves, but it would not be with the same time I had previously wasted. As a freelance writer, editor, publisher, and playwright, I was all over the place in my life. The very thing I had suspected about the subject of structure turned out to mirror the lack of it in my own life. I am literally my own administrative assistant, customer service representative, researcher, receptionist, quote generator, manuscript reviewer, and obviously editor, writer, and publisher. I was in for an awakening and subsequent hard work to be performed because I juggle so many hats.

In my journey through mastering Dr. Bush's prescription for a structured life, I realized many things. I realized that my vision needed *transcription*; I needed to write my vision and make it plain (Habakkuk 2:2). My time also needed an *assignment*; I needed to make a plan and walk that plan out. I needed to assign my time each day to accomplish what was before me. I needed to be diligent in fulfilling what was expected of me; with my clients, my family, and within my own personal life. My relationships needed *defining*; I came to the realization that some people are in my life for a reason, season, or lifetime. Those who had come to the end of their purpose in my life, it was okay for them to move on and live out their own purpose. I even discovered that one relationship was preventing me from reaching new levels.

My money needed a mission; I had to assign each dollar a specific task in order to maximize its purpose. These life-changing ideas challenged me to examine why I fall short many months or why my dollars are not performing to their full potential. My faith needed a definite *goal and chief aim;* I had to work my faith with action and I had to aim high! My confessions needed *restriction;* I had to hone in on what I confessed; knowingly and unknowingly and give or not give it purpose in my life. My thoughts needed to be tried; this area of my life had gotten out of control. I had to re-track my entire thought processes and practice positive counter- thoughts when a negative thought tried to align itself with difficult life circumstances. This is one of life's most difficult things to do; however, I knew that once mastered, there would be nothing I could not accomplish! Finally, my emotions needed to be *weighed*; this subject was in need of structure too. This area doesn't only apply to people who are overly emotional; it also applies to those, like me, who try to avoid emotions which can become a hindrance. I knew I had to quickly apply and master structure in my life.

To the casual reader, *STRUCTURE* will be an extremely informative, step-by-step, and straightforward guide to organizing life. Dr. Bush uses practical exercises from which each reader can conduct self-examinations and assessments to help him/her move beyond average or below average to one of structure and success. The knowledge and expertise Dr. Bush gained by walking out each step is evident and graces every paragraph of *STRUCTURE.*

Structuring one's life might seem to be a daunting task. However, one must commit to the work to reap the reward. *"Structure: The Master Key to KINGDOM Success consist of scriptural disciplines referred to as "ingredients" necessary for integrating the use of efforts into one unified force that will make us consistently, effectively, and purposefully fulfilled each day."* (Dr. Finace Bush)

This remarkable book is a how-to-succeed roadmap that leads to a structured life, all rolled into one. However, you must be prepared; it is the "cutting edge" many of us need to propel us to the next level of organized living. It will no doubt become a daily manual and resource for readers who have an interest in moving beyond "mediocrity."

Dr. Bush, thank you for opening up to us the last twenty years of your life and detailing them in such a practical, comprehensive way so that we, too, may avoid your pitfalls and retrace the proven successes in your life. To the millions of readers who will turn the pages of the book, the blueprint for success has already been laid; you simply need to follow it to reach your full potential and live out your God-given purpose. So, roll up your sleeves, get your note pad, be honest with yourself, dig in, and prepare for your next level!

Carmen Santos Monteiro is a freelance writer, editor, playwright, and former English and Writing skills instructor for a local community college. She writes business and entertainment articles, blogs, and other online media and has written faith-based magazine articles for Kenneth Copeland Ministries and others. Among her credits are book projects for Dr. Creflo Dollar, Taffi Dollar, Ruben Studdard, and others. She is the author of "Side Gig", "Blood Stains," and other faith-based materials. She is passionate about teaching others how to produce multiple streams of income in their lives and encouraging them to create the lifestyle they desire. She is the mother of three beautiful children.

Carmen Santos Monteiro
(404) 348.4963
CarmenSantosMonteiro@gmail.com

EIGHT INGREDIENTS OF "STRUCTURE"

Volume 1

My **VISION** needs TRANSCRIPTION

My **TIME** needs an ASSIGNMENT

My **RELATIONSHIPS** need DEFINING

My **MONEY** needs a MISSION

My **FAITH** needs a DEFINITE GOAL and a CHIEF AIM

My **CONFESSIONS** need RESTRICTIONS

My **THOUGHTS** need to be TRIED

My **EMOTIONS** need to be WEIGHED

The **PROFIT** of the Earth is for **ALL!**
(Ecclesiastes 5:9)

Let's begin by acknowledging that the Holy writings indicate "The profit of the earth is for all" and is accessible to everyone who properly applies themselves to what the Creator left us. The impact of this verse should be felt immediately because it clarifies God's purpose for the earth's abundant supply of resources. If all things produced by the earth were distributed to all men equally there would be more than enough for everyone.

When we view this statement from a perspective of the inheritance God prepared for all humanity to enjoy, it exposes the fact that many diligent persons enjoy the comforts of earth because of their aggressive pursuit of a better tomorrow. While on the other hand, many slothful persons remain without earth's comforts because they are disoriented, dysfunctional, and disenfranchised.

Many people are bound to complacency through ignorance, which subjects them to a spirit of mediocrity. Wherever mediocrity exists the ability to accept non-progressive people and systems as they are will continue to erode that division of society and eventually prevail towards its non-existence.

On the other hand a hidden "profit" that earth affords everyone is realized when we use our earth time as a wise investment for eternity. This is the greater purpose that the Creator intended from the beginning. What we plant or sow in our earthly life will determine what we harvest or reap now and in eternity.

We must realize that there is more to life than what is going on here and now in the earth realm. We are a spirit that has a soul that lives in a body. Our body is not who we really are but is an earth-suit we wear while on Earth. This is so that we can exchange with earthly vessels like ourselves and all other forms of Earth's habitation.

Keep this in mind, the Earth we live on is subject to a time-line, however, we are eternal creatures from a heavenly realm that uses our time to advance our eternal existence. Although the profitability of the earth is accessible to us, our most profitable endeavor on earth is to prepare ourselves for eternity.

Table of Contents

STRUCTURE

Dedication and Acknowledgments V

The 8 Ingredients of Structure..XI

Volume 1

The PROFIT of the Earth is for ALL! XII

Introduction

A significant book..XIX

CHAPTER 1

Structure Begins With Right Foundation 1

A New Spirit Started Developing in Me...................................... 13

Chapter 1 Review and Action Plan... 18

CHAPTER 2

Working Out Your Salvation.. 40

Faith Begins Where the Will of God is Known.......................... 46

The Will of God is not Automatic.. 49

Soteria: The Privileges of Salvation 53

The power of the second birth 54

The Truth is 59

CHAPTER 3

Social Malpractice.. 63

God Births New Beginnings From Strange Encounters 67

Self-discovery is the Key to Personal Fulfillment...................... 68

How We Function Best 68

Our Best Example 69

Failed Attempts: Striving Without Priorities 72

Uniqueness Requires Attention..74

An Experiment That Paid Dividends..75

Social Malpractice Self Enrichment Lesson 79

CHAPTER 4

The Power of the Pattern..82

Success Simplified: The Power of the Pattern............................86

Predestined and Guaranteed Success...87

The Key to Joshua's Ministry: An Old Testament Example......88

Striving for a Mastery 90

CHAPTER 5

The Curse of Mediocrity..95

Other Diabolical Satanic Effects of Mediocrity 99

A Lesson from the Comics..102

Understanding Crisis...104

Paul's Perspective...105

Mind Blindness 107

Life Without Proper Orientation..108

Winning Over Mediocrity by Implementing Structure.............110

Mediocrity is a State of Mind 111

Noah Example...112

The Ark of Provision...112

Let's Be Real!..113

Understanding Faith..113

The Process 114

CHAPTER 6

Prioritizing My Tri-une or Three-part Man 116

From the Owner's Manual Perspective 117

The Natural Man Must be Forced into Submission 119

Your Mind Must be Renewed and Your Affections

set on High Things 122

Importance of Orientation.. 122

Mind Renewal Begins With Orientation 123

The Seven Components to Structure 127

The Process 129

Air Beaters... 130

A meaningful struggle in context.. 131

The Power of Advice 135

How Information Gets in the Mix 137

Eight Ingredients of "Structure" 141

My **VISION** needs TRANSCRIPTION

My **TIME** needs an ASSIGNMENT

My **RELATIONSHIPS** need DEFINING

My **MONEY** needs a MISSION

My **FAITH** needs a DEFINITE GOAL and a CHIEF AIM

My **CONFESSIONS** need RESTRICTIONS

My **THOUGHTS** need to be TRIED

My **EMOTIONS** need to be WEIGHED

CHAPTER 7

The Use of Laws and Principles 142

The Importance of Structured Disciplines.................................. 145

Striving for a Crown 149

CHAPTER 8

My Vision Needs Transcription 150

The Cornerstone to a Prosperous Life 151

CHAPTER 9

It All Begins With Time 161

The Cost of Mistaken Perception 169

Time Needs Assignment in Business...................... 169

TIME ZONES 172

CHAPTER 10

I Must Understand Relationships........................... 174

My Relationships Need Defining 174

"Love Trouble".. 175

Easier to fall in Love than Stay in Love 175

Three Primary Principles 178

Problem with Perceptions 181

Keeping The Leverage of Love is Possible............. 183

The First Principle: Making Love and Relationships Last! 183

The Importance of the Nine Fruits of the Spirit 186

Measuring Your Relationships................................ 187

The Way of Love: Primary laws of relationships.... 189

Historical Evolution of Relationships..................... 200

Becoming fit for relationships................................ 216

Unforgiveness; a Signal of Love 224

CHAPTER 11

Next, I Must Understand....................................... 226

Money Answers and Defends 228
Having Money is Like Not Having a Toothache! 229
Questions to help you start realignment................................231
A Faithful Steward 236
How We Handle Money Reveals Our Priorities and Values
More Proof God Wants To Prosper You..................................239
God Supplies Givers so They Have Seed for Sowing 240
How the "Grace" of God abounds 242
Money with a Mission 249
Planning Your Financial Mission...253

CHAPTER 12
My Faith Needs a Definite Aim and a Chief Goa 255
Related passages and encouragements for edification...........269
Bibliography 275

Introduction

A significant book

I began this project with the assumption of the responsibility to motivate Believers to re-examine their lives through Scripture from the perspective of God's creative purpose for our existence. I had a burden and conviction that the Holy Spirit birthed in me through prayer, study, and observation of the conflict that Satan subtly plants both in the world and the church to divide and conquer.

There are many types of motivational and self-help books that assist secular society to succeed and are readily embraced by the religious community and viewed as effective tools for life. Yet, in many of the same religious circles, the words **"Christian success or prosperous Christians"** are viewed more negatively. This type of ignorance makes Kingdom bonding and Kingdom expansion difficult to realize.

The desire for exposing the Christian community to a combination of proven, practical truths, destroying myths, and heresies implanted by enemies of faith, is factored heavily throughout this work. Also, my desire to establish a clear pathway for Christian success through simple obedience to God's Word was equally important.

God wants each of His children to understand where and how they fit in His master plan. According to Genesis 1:26, we were created in the image and likeness of God, but we lost our true identity through Adam's sin. As we rediscover our identity through Christ, we are reconciled to our privileges and rights to operate as His sons.

Notice, John 1:12, *"But to as many as did receive Him, He gave the authority (power, privilege, and right) to become the children of God, that is, to those who believe in (adhere to, trust in, and rely on) His name--"* (AMP)

We must no longer continue to accept a lifestyle of defeat because we wear the badge of Christianity. Neither shall we stoop to poverty and depravity to suggest a false humility to a world that cannot comprehend spiritual truths. These grossly flawed perspectives are not acceptable nor do they represent our Father's will. They only serve the purpose of permeating the insignificant lifestyle of mediocrity that leaves most Believers without influence among their peers.

Notice the emphasis Jesus placed on the power and necessity of Heaven's influence in this world's system, as expressed in Matthew 5:13-16. *"You are the salt of the earth; but if the salt loses its flavor, how shall it be seasoned? It is then good for nothing but to be thrown out and trampled underfoot by men. You are the light of the world. A city that is set on a hill cannot be hidden. Nor do they light a lamp and put it under a basket, but on a lampstand, and it gives light to all who are in the house. Let your light so shine before men, that they may see your good works and glorify your Father in heaven."* (NKJV)

Clearly these statements from Jesus himself illustrates the need for Kingdom citizens to have primary influence, power, and authority in both the world's system and His Kingdom, so that every transaction in the earth realm is a reflection of Heaven.

In Paul's letter to the Colossians 4:5, 6, he compels the Believers in the same manner to, *"Walk in wisdom toward those who are outside, redeeming the time. Let your speech always be with grace, seasoned with salt, that you may know how you ought to answer each one."* (NKJV)

Also, Luke 2:52, states that, *"And Jesus increased in wisdom and stature, and in favour with God and man."* His growth in both realms which resulted in favor with both systems is evident in this passage and throughout the gospels, which illustrates the need to hold ourselves accountable to the demonstration of His example.

We have a great responsibility as Christians to win as many souls as we can from this world for Christ. Therefore, each of us as Kingdom citizens who "no longer belong to ourselves," have a personal duty to "ponder the path of our feet and let all our ways be established," (Proverbs 4:26). This is the surefire route to a successful, purposeful, prosperous, and fulfilling life of Christ-likeness or Kingdom influence.

Structure: The Master Key to Success consist of **scriptural disciplines** referred to as ingredients necessary for integrating the use of our efforts into one unified force that will make us consistently, effectively, and purposefully fulfilled each day.

Perhaps you lack a decisive internal core regarding your God-given purpose and personal mission, your occupation, role in society or how you relate to family, friends, and associates. Perhaps you have a good job but hate the work, or maybe you are someone who daily juggles a lot of things but don't derive any real joy or fulfillment from doing them.

It is time for us to realize that we were created from "God-stock" and "God-stock" is supremely victorious in all things. Understanding the power of transformation through mind renewal, using the Word of God, is the crucial link that adds the insight needed to balance our lives.

Notice how Ephesians 1:11, 12 expresses the fact that God makes all things correspond to His purpose *"according to the **counsel of His will"**,* which demonstrates the decisive measure He uses to sustain the universal logic of all past, present, and future creations. *"In Him also we have obtained an inheritance, being predestined **according to the purpose** of Him who **worketh all things after the counsel of His own will:** That we should be to the praise of His glory, who first trusted in Christ."*

My aim is to convey the importance of each, being aware of having an internal compass. A compass drafted from our understanding of our God-given purpose. It also supervises and directs our decisions, gifts, skills, relations, activities, and plans according to the counsel of our will to ensure a wholesome life.

This type of revelation frees us from an un-tested, dominated-felt life, and the need to live assumptive and opinionated. We will not become like cynics and skeptics who are miserable and cannot see above the logic that drives their lifestyle choices.

I am extremely excited for the readers of this book. I hope that my ten years of journaling and twenty-five years of principal insights will attract the masses of potential achievers who may have been deceived about God's true perspective of success.

As you read this book, I pray that you will keep an open mind, read prayerfully, reexamine the material against the Scriptures and allow the Spirit of God to confirm your way.

CHAPTER

1

STRUCTURE BEGINS WITH RIGHT FOUNDATION

Masonry is a popular home-building craft and has a remarkable durability that is appreciated when all the regulations and requirements for a particular structure are met. While few of us imagine that our homes will exist for centuries, when we choose masonry we're choosing a material that has precisely that capability.

Masonry is popular for many reasons, including its beauty, versatility and resistance to fire, earthquakes and sound transmission. Let's not forget masonry's remarkable durability that is appreciated when the requirements in a particular structure are met. While few of us think that our homes will exist for centuries, when we choose masonry, we choose building materials that has precisely that ability.

Some of the world's most vulnerable masonry structures are the Taj Mahal, the Egyptian Pyramids, the Coliseums in Rome, and the Great Sphinx of Giza have awed generations of people because of their ability to withstand time. Like masonry, the Holy Scriptures are more than able to make us wise. In conjunction with the Holy Spirit, Scriptures give us information and empowerment to work with, and make repairs to, personal areas of our lives; the kind of repairs that enable us to withstand normal tests and trials of life.

Notice, the words of Jesus, *"It is the Spirit that **gives life**, He is the life giver; the flesh conveys no benefit or profit at all. The **words** that I speak unto you **are spirit, and they are life"**,* John 6:63. Each of us should be concerned about whether we are building on the proper foundation by applying God's confirmable truths that give us the correct way to live.

A phrase that you will see repeated throughout these pages is found in Proverbs 16:25, *"There is a way that seems right to a man, but ends in multiple ways of death."* Now let's begin this journey of reconstruction together.

BUILDING ON THE RIGHT FOUNDATION

Notice the implication of Psalm 11:3, *"If the foundations are destroyed. What can the righteous do?"*

What is a foundation and why is it important to have one? Or, to make this more relevant; why do you do what you do and who or what influences the direction of your life? Are you living in a self-defeating cycle of frustration and chaos? Is it good to impress and appease others at the expense of your personal peace and power? Last but not least, who told you or what makes you think you've discovered the appropriate way to live?

Webster defines a "foundation" as the base on which something rest; or, the basis for which something exist; specifically the supporting part of a wall, house, relationship, system, reality, etc., and at least partially underground, the **fundamental principle on which something is founded.** It is the basis or standard; a supporting material or part beneath an outer part, as a foundational garment.

Greek nouns THEMELIOS or THEMELION denotes a thing, a standard, a principle or a system upon which something is built. It is used as a noun, with *lithos*; a stone. Herein lies the acid test to determine if our practices and habits are correctly established on the correct foundation.

If an action or reaction in which you engage constantly leaves you without internal peace or rest, you need to examine it or weigh it against the truth. What's happening to you may not be the problem, but how you handle it may be in need of change!

Many times we handle our affairs according to *what seems right* to us instead of what is appropriate [or the standard] for a situation. Here is something we should always remember; that which we consider *normal* usually determines the **importance** we place on it. Our definition of normalcy was probably shaped through the experiences of our developmental years, which may or may not have included God.

Things that are **important** to us are only important because they meet our *standards*; our *standards* impact and shape the perimeters [broad or narrow, right or wrong] of the way we believe and the things in which we believe. Our *beliefs* reside in our conscience which is the place where "strong-holds" are erected that form our deep seated *convictions*.

Ultimately our *convictions*, referred to by Webster as "strong beliefs, or opinions", are the forces that work together to drive our *responses*.

This process influences our behaviors regardless of whether they are right or wrong. This is the single reason the standard for every operation needs to be tested against "truth."

If you are in any way like I was before I began this journey, testing your beliefs and practices against "truth" will divinely inspire you. You might see changes in your thought processes and habits that have developed over your life-span.

Whenever our convictions drive our responses, we are usually inflexible about the position we take whether it is correct or not. The problem is that we may have settled with the wrong frame of mind. The way we handle our personal issues and other people will, to a great extent, determine the quality and happiness of our lives.

This brings me to a very important point

In Proverbs 4:26, we are advised to *"Ponder and consider well the path of our feet, and **let all of our ways** be established and ordered alright.* This passage suggests that there is an established route [foundational measure] for every way we might chose to take in this life. But in most cases we may not have "pondered and considered well...."

In other words we must act considerately in *all* we do by **"putting the word of God on one scale, and what we have done or what** we are about to do on the other scale to see how they agree." Be critical in examining if your way is good before God because this will determine whether it will end well. Do nothing rashly!

One reason Jesus commanded that we seek God's Kingdom and righteousness first is to help us weigh our actions and thoughts against the appropriate way [foundational measure] of fully living life. Note, *"But seek (aim at and strive after) first of all His kingdom and His righteousness (His way of doing and being right), and then all these things taken together will be given you besides." (Matthew 6:33, AMP)*

Another reason to seek the Kingdom is to prevent us from incurring God's wrath which shall be revealed against ALL ungodliness and unrighteousness.

We cannot pick and choose the part of righteousness we will prioritize, because God expects us to honor all of His sayings regardless of how it feels or what we think. Notice how the Apostle Paul addressed this issue to the Believers in Rome.

"For the wrath of God is revealed from Heaven against all *ungodliness* and *unrighteousness* of men, who hold the truth in unrighteousness, because what may be known of God is manifest in them, for God has shown it to them. For since the creation of the world His invisible *attributes* are clearly seen, being understood by the things that are made, *even* His eternal power and Godhead, **so that they are without excuse.**," (Romans 1:18-20)

It is Important to Know That Some Foundational Things Have Been Kept Secret

The secret things of God do not interfere with our ability to live successful lives. I'll discuss this thoroughly in chapter two.

Jesus stated in Matthew 13:35, "that it might be fulfilled which was spoken by the prophets, saying: *"I will open My mouth in parables; I will **utter things which have been kept secret** from the **foundation** of the world."* Isn't it interesting that God has kept some **"foundational things"** secret although they are the fundamental principles upon which activities both in Heaven and Earth rest?

YOU MUST CORRECT YOUR FOUNDATION

In Luke 6:48-49, notice how *The Message* Bible addresses the process of correction and the importance of a "right foundation". *"**If you work the words into your life,** you are like a smart carpenter who dug deep and laid the foundation of his house on bedrock. When the river burst its banks and crashed against the house, **nothing could shake it;** it was built to last.*

*But if you just use my words in Bible studies and **don't work them into your life,** you are like a dumb carpenter who built a house but skipped the foundation. When the swollen river came crashing in, **it collapsed** like a house of cards. It was a total loss."*

The *Amplified* further clarifies the need for right foundation using the same passages, *"For everyone who comes to Me and listens to My words [in order to heed their teaching] and does them, I will show you what he is like. He is like a man building a house, **who dug and went** *down deep and laid a foundation upon the rock; and when a flood arose, the torrent broke against that house and **could not shake or move** it, because it had been securely built or founded on a rock.*

*But he who merely **hears and does not practice** doing My words is like a man who built a house on the ground without a foundation, against which the torrent burst, and immediately it collapsed and fell, and the breaking and **ruin of that house was great.**"*

It is obvious from the focus of each version that when we fail to investigate the values, standards, and beliefs that govern our decision-making processes, our lives may be subject to collapse and ruin. Again, Proverbs 16, reads *"There is a way that seems right to a man,* [because it is most logical to him] *but the end there of are the ways of death."*

There are two general types of concrete failure which are also similar to our human experience: They are structural and surface. **Structural failure** usually results from outside forces like freezing water; and **Surface damage** most often is caused by improper finishing techniques or concrete mixtures that do not have the right ratio of something as simple as water
to cement.

Until we are aware of the fact that our way of processing and determining is flawed and problematic, there is a possibility we will repeatedly make the same mistakes. Both structural [foundational] and surface [finishing] problems will continue to interfere with our ability to live a successful life with continuity.

Kingdom systems take an uncommon approach to power, peace, prosperity, and progress, because they are based on principles not practices. When we understand the principles, we can create effective practices. Notice how the wise man Solomon attempts to advance us through his insightful understanding of how a life should be properly set up.

*Through skillful and godly **Wisdom** is a house, a life, a home, or a family built, and by **understanding** it is established on a sound and good foundation, and by **knowledge** shall its chambers of every area be filled with all precious and pleasant riches. A wise man is strong and is better than a strong man and a man of knowledge increases and strengthens his power; For by wise counsel you can wage your war, and in an abundance of counselors there is victory and safety. **Wisdom** is too high for a fool: He opens not his mouth in the gate.* **Proverbs 24:3-7**

I'm beginning with the last verse of this quote because it speaks directly to the description of a weak man who, for whatever reason, has decided to live as though wisdom is too high for him. He may not be aware of the daily cost to him resulting from his unchecked ways of assessing and evaluating his own practices against God's Word. His despairing way of thinking convinces him to refuse to take pains in the pursuit of the one resource without which God, His Creator, never attempted to accomplish anything. And that one thing is WISDOM.

So he sits down *"In the seat of the scornful,"* persecuting right methods and applications because of the blindness of his own heart. He foolishly remains content without wisdom, as though he has no capacity for it. Therefore the advantages he has for getting wisdom are all in vain to him.

His way is *"right in his own eyes"* without a confirmed alignment with truth; he is both judge and jury for those who differentiate from his course.

It is no easy thing to get wisdom but everyone must be willing to pay the price for it. Those of us who lead and are responsible for others in any capacity must use wisdom. It is a foolish thing when leaders are slothful and remiss in pursuit of the wisdom that corresponds with God's standards for living. So we are better equipped to lead others according to what is right by God's guidelines instead of our assumptions.

Assumption is not just the lowest form of knowledge it can also be the device of self deceit that makes an individual vulnerable to wrong influences and positions with important people and issues. Both, Jeremiah and Paul, warned us to not be victimized by the deceitfulness of our own heart which can alienate an individual from God through shallow thinking and limited, untested imagination.

I speak not to fools and certainly you who are reading this material are not as fools who spend the quantity of their time in sport, entertainment, and pleasures more than in preparation for the service of your call and purpose.

I submit here that all leaders and young people should take pains to get wisdom so they may have a good reputation and be qualified for public business.

Note, when people neglect to prepare themselves properly for their own causes, that failure to prepare leaves a person unfit for service and ignorant of the measures necessary to advance causes, which councils or magistrates would heed.

Such a person will not be fit for representation because he would not have pursued that which is necessary to escape the deceitful experiences and shallow reasons of his own heart.

This is why King Solomon advised, saying, *"Get wisdom, get understanding: forget it not; neither decline from its words. Forsake her not, and she shall preserve you: Love her, and she shall keep you. Wisdom Is the principle thing; therefore get **wisdom**: and with all thy getting get **understanding**."* (Proverbs 4:5-7)

Always remember that life does not yield wisdom just to reward our existence. Wisdom must be prioritized and pursued in order to obtain it.

PERSONAL DISCOVERY THROUGH "STRUCTURE"

Over the course of my life, I have tried many concepts and strategies attempting to maximize my effectiveness. However, the one thing that continued to show up in my journals was a lack of continuity. Getting started had never been my problem. **Keeping momentum**, for lack of a better term, is the hurdle that kept me in bondage to mediocrity.

Like the Apostle Paul, *"to will was present with me, but how to perform I could not find.* I always had good intentions and urge to do, ***but lacked the power (missing key) to carry it out."*** (Romans 7:18)

A REVELATION OF MYSELF
THAT EMPOWERED MY WILL

I was tired of not following through with many of the endeavors I would start. While praying in the Spirit one morning, a light turned on inside of me. The Holy Spirit began speaking about my need to develop a **spirit of persistence**. Apparently, at that time in my life, the focus of my goals was not adequate to sustain my endurance or drive.

I began examining my most passionate desires and narrowing my focus which enabled me to **define my purpose**. Laboring with my purpose enabled me to craft and **write out specific and clearly defined plans** which, in turn, strengthened my confidence. Sharing my excitement with others helped me realize the importance of **shielding myself from negative influences**. Then the Holy Spirit led me to **form covenant alliances** with persons willing to demand my accountability and encourage follow through.

The absence of this one quality kept me from accomplishing my goals. A few days later in a vision, God gave me a master key that enabled me to define myself, identify my purpose, establish an inner core of disciplines, and write a mission for my existence.

The Holy Spirit said "You lack structure!" That is the master key to your success.

Breaking deeply imbedded habits that caused me to procrastinate and give up on projects and tasks was very difficult for me initially. I would start strongly and passionately but **lose focus** because my most important actions did not correspond with my goals. My inability to

say no and my **lack of commitment** to my own dreams made me a "sitting duck" for distractions from people who had **no value of time or goals for their future.** I did not know what to do to break this self-defeating cycle. While I was viewed as a helper to others, I would find myself in a crowd of people and feeling lonely because I was not being fulfilled.

So, one morning after my time of worship and praying in the spirit, I began meditating on 1Corinthians. 9:25-27 and Joshua 1:8. Finally, near the end of my devotion the Holy Spirit spoke to me saying, **"You lack structure! That is your missing ingredient and master key to success."**

Over the course of the next few days, I gave thought and study to what was revealed. It became obvious to me that I needed to **arrange important daily functions by prioritizing them to correspond with my goals.** As I prayed for wisdom, the Holy Spirit continued clarifying and translating my purpose into a plan of action.

With this new enlightenment I was beginning to see more clearly. Each day as the light became brighter I began receiving "structure" in the form of principles of discipline that constructed a clear pathway to a strong, effective, purposeful, well-balanced Christian life.

Throughout the first several weeks of visitations, the following eight disciplines were revealed to me in four categories: **Categories 1 and 2:** My **Time** needs an Assignment; My **Relationships** needs Defining, and **Categories 3 and 4:** My **Devotion** needs Persistence and My **Change** needs Insistence.

As I defined each key discipline, it became more obvious to me that the reason I constantly failed to accomplish my endeavors was due to a lack of structure. It also became clear to me why so many others who are highly gifted, talented, and scholastic have difficulty making their dreams become reality.

To live without structured priorities was disastrous for me. Each day, I began with the intentions of making my life better only to discover by the day's end that I had allowed another pearl to get away. Like so many others, **I would drift from day-to-day as if I had an agreement with time to wait on me. In the meantime, my foolish malpractices** and lack of adequate priorities left me continually empty and frustrated.

Like one of my favorite writers, Og Mandino, "Tomorrow I will begin, I told myself day-after-day. I didn't know then, that tomorrow is only found in the calendars of fools." Blind to my foolish faults, I was wasting my life in deliberation for I knew not what, and I would have procrastinated until it was too late had it not been for the Holy Spirit giving me these keys.

The structure keys were first a daily planning log to manage my daily functions so that I could focus on increasing my effectiveness. Immediately, I began experiencing a more fulfilled life. As I became more conscious, I began to realize the amount of time I was wasting on sports programs and other insignificant activities that created added obstacles and distractions.

A NEW SPIRIT STARTED DEVELOPING IN ME

A sense of **"Destiny"** had seemingly been imparted to me. I became hungry, alert, and conscious of my surroundings and the actions I needed to take in order to remain focused and persistent. I begin taking control of each day, without allowing changing situations and challenges to dominate me. This actually felt like being born again, again! Man, I was really alive again! I was revived and filled with vision and a clear mission.

I also had an abundance of energy and enthusiasm to accomplish my priorities. With this key I knew I was ready to conquer the world. Now I understand; now I get it.

Fresh Revelation is **Fresh** Anointing!

Fresh Anointing is **Fresh** Power!

Fresh Power is **Fresh** Ability; God's Grace!

The grace that accommodates the "Spirit of Revelation" is empowerment to accomplish and succeed in every endeavor inspired by God. This is an encouraging expression that echoes in my spirit each day I enter into my morning devotion.

I have always held the conviction that God never gives us **responsibility** without giving us the **ability [grace]** to carry it out. But, many times my personal struggles left me vulnerable to continual distractions that hindered me from the completion of important daily tasks.

My life had no significant structure to enable consistent effectiveness. I finally realized that life is a maze for anyone who cannot define their purpose and **lacks the discipline to prioritize**. While I appeared to be an accomplished pastor and professional artist, my identity crises subjected me to constant frustration and defeat.

As a leader I had to acknowledge that **attempting to reconstruct a life is a very difficult task or challenge.** I desperately needed to go through the process of gaining mastery over my personal struggles if I were to succeed in assisting others with their struggles.

Like the Apostle Paul, I had to learn how to; *"keep my body disciplined, to bring it into subjection: for fear that after proclaiming the things pertaining to the gospel to others. I myself should become unfit, not being able to stand the test, and be rejected as a counterfeit."*

Life's decisions are perplexed when one does not know where, or how to begin especially if the individual is unable to discern the most important step to take first. The wrong perspective of God, people and things, along with the absence of vision, purpose, and self-awareness might keep an individual stuck in a self-defeating cycle. This deceitful cycle consist of a pattern of thoughts and actions that continue to produce more of the pain and discomfort from which we may desire to be free.

Living daily like this can become difficult. In my case, for many years I was too stubborn to change, and I was addicted to doing things the same way in spite of my many failures. I had an **illusion of safety in familiarity.**

NEW LIGHT!

Now life is being revealed to me in a new light. This new **revelation** started generating increased personal ability and power to accomplish my aspirations. Paul described this ability we receive from God as:

*"Precious treasure, the **divine light** of the Gospel that **we possess** in [our] earthen vessels that the excellence, exceeding greatness of the power may be shown to be **of God** and **not from ourselves**"* (2 Corinthians 4:7)

In other words, it's not by our strength or ability that we accomplish great things, but by God's Spirit. *"Not by might, nor by power, but by my Spirit, says the Lord of hosts."* (Zechariah 4:6)

Through this, my desire began to stimulate a sense of urgency and purpose within me. A new light was turned on inside of me that made me take responsibility for my successes and failures. This new light enabled me to understand that **the Word of God expresses two major categories of successful living: 1.** Success attained by striving to enter into a better and more abundant tomorrow. **2.** Success attained by one's ability to accept things as they are without internal conflict or competing desires. I will discuss these two ideas by using "categories" to make it easier to follow.

First, let's discuss category 1. The difference between those who are successful and those who are the failures in this group may be that the *successful persons keep applying themselves* even when the *risks* are high. They develop a routine through persistence that turns into momentum. They major in the *possibilities* not the risks. But, on the other hand, those who fail in this group usually stop applying themselves whenever **risks** surface. They major in the **risk** instead of the possibilities.

MISINTERPRETATION OF THE RISK FACTOR

Many people fail to understand that **risk** actually **determines** the **value** a person places on a thing or the benefit of accomplishing a goal. The more value I place on the goal or the thing, the more I am willing to take the risk. The less value it holds, the less likely we are to take the risk.

Value-driven desire is the **fuel** to **persistence** that enables a person to hurdle over **risk** when it is part of the process. In some cases, it is not that people identified as failures are true to the definition of failure, but they simply fail to place value on the things they desire to accomplish due to fear of personal risk or failure.

So let's define **personal risk** as, *the things we don't want to be affected by processes that we are uncertain of because we never experienced them. Or, to have an abundance of uncertainty about the changes that may occur in personal relationships, financial stability, savings, diet, [eating habits], schedules, and many other things that rank high on a person's priority list.*

Here's an example, this can be **explained by comparing**; the woman with the issue of blood identified in Mark 5:25-28, with the young rich ruler mentioned in Matthew 19:16-22. The woman with the issue **valued** her **deliverance above** the **risk of losing** all she had, but the young rich ruler **valued** his personal **withholdings** above the **risk** of getting delivered, and experiencing fulfillment on God's terms.

Now let's look at Category 2: Success accomplished by one's ability to accept things as they are, without internal conflict or competing desires. This group can be divided into the **content** and the **miserable**.

The **Content**, are those who experience consistent internal peace that balances their **effort** with their **expectations** each day. They live within the comforts of their own conscience without competing desires despite daily challenges or exposure to better, more modern, or abundant things.

For them, *"godliness with contentment is a great gain."* They accept what they are given expecting no more or less and they are always content with such things as they have. **As it is written** in the epistle of Romans 14:22, *"Happy is he who does not condemn himself in what he approves."* **A few examples** are teenagers and adults who are not compelled to get a driver's license, move out on their own, buy a car, or pursue a career.

Now the **Miserable** in this category are not hard to identify because often their day ends without them being any closer to the change they desire to make, goals they want to accomplish, or finishing tasks they intended to complete.

Their **pretended contentment** is driven by the **fear of not being able** to compete, accomplish, or complete a task to some other person's satisfaction. Their fears and insecurities cause them to pretend to be content so they are not pressured to attempt something and fail. They are **afraid to fail** so they refuse to try.

I will further explore the word **"afraid"** and the primary "fears" we must master that I discuss in the upcoming chapter, "Mastering FEAR."

CHAPTER 1 REVIEW AND ACTION PLAN

Building upon the right foundation, self-enrichment lesson

1. According to Proverbs 16:25, *"There is a way that seems right to a man, but ends in multiple ways of death"*.

    As it pertains to your life, list two "ways" that may have seemed right to you (at the time) and if you had not made a change they would have ended in destruction or death.

    _____

    _____

    _____

    _____

2. If a(n) _____ or reaction you engage constantly leaves you without _____ or rest, you need to _____ _____ it or weigh it _____ the _____.

    What's _____ to you may not be your problem, but how _____ are _____ may need to _____!

3. What are some required components that a Kingdom citizen needs to build a foundation? Use Scripture references.

    _____

    _____

    _____

    _____

4. Why is it important to have a foundation? Luke 6:48-49 (The Message) says, "If you work the words into your life, you are like a smart carpenter who *dug deep and laid the foundation* of his

house on bedrock. When the river burst its banks and crashed against the house, nothing could shake it; it was *built to last.*

_____

_____

_____

_____

5. What are the detriments to a person not having a proper foundation?

_____

_____

_____

_____

6. According to Proverbs 24:3-7, how can you avoid spiritual *structural failure* and *surface damage?*

_____

_____

_____

_____

7. Refer to Romans 7:18, what are some of the challenges you have that keep you from being effective?

_____

_____

_____

_____

8. Read your answers from number six above and determine which challenge you are willing to change immediately and write a plan of

action to overcome that challenge.

_____

_____

_____

_____

9. Take a moment to fill in the blanks then openly repeat each ingredient.

    a. My _____ needs an assignment.

    b. My _____ needs defining.

    c. My _____ needs persistence.

    d. My _____ needs insistence.

10. Based on what you have read and learned so far, how will you personally benefit from incorporating structure into your life?

    _____

    _____

    _____

    _____

11. This book introduced two major categories of successful living:

    a. The statement, "Success by striving to enter into a better and more abundant tomorrow" describes people who major in the _____ and not the _____.

    Failure happens when people major in the _____ instead of the _____.

    b. Success accomplished by ones' ability to accept things as they are without _____

    or

Daily thought and meditation
Fresh Revelation is **Fresh** Anointing!
Fresh Anointing is **Fresh** Power!
Fresh Power is **Fresh** Ability and God's Grace!

SUCCESS

This is the most important issue we will likely deal with in this lifetime is success. The Holy Spirit once whispered to me that "many people are consumed with life but not learning how to live it." Although God has provided a door to life, many of His children still prefer to live by their own measures: guessing, experimenting, or simply following the way of the masses. All the while, they suffer great pain and agony at the hand of their own decisions.

The Holy Scriptures make it clear that *"The way of life is not in man"* despite how it appears from our own way of viewing things. When we attempt to exist in this life apart from God, our Creator, without His Word as our standard for living, every way is right in our own eyes. Solomon stated in Proverbs 3:7, *"Do not be wise in your own eyes; Fear the LORD and depart from evil."*

John 10:1-10 exposes Jesus as both the key and the combination to "True life." Clearly the solution is to enter in the right door. In John 8:12, Jesus reemphasized that *"He is the light which is life"*; after He convicted the conscience of those who judged the woman found in adultery. These are only two of the many accounts that confirm John 1:4, which states that *"in Him was Life and the Life was the Light of men,"* which is to say the **light** [correct instructions for living] was in the **life** [Zoe, Greek.for the God kind of life]. In other words, the proper way to live is in the principles Jesus subjected His life to because "the life was in the light" and not in the way of the "thief"; trickery.

"SALVATION THE TRUE FOUNDATION OF LIFE"

In the Gospel of Matthew 7:21-27, Jesus taught an important lesson regarding the single most important priority in life.

Although society may have decided that the practice of Christianity is no more essential than brands of religions throughout the world, it is a clear indication that Satan's schemes are working in the lives of unbelievers. They have reduced the born- again experience to a religious ritual rather than a relational reconnection to Jehovah; the only true and living God, Father and Creator of the universe. The sacred writings (Holy Scriptures) establish four exclusive truths that all men must recognize:

1. **There is only one God;** *"There is one God and one mediator between God and men, the Man Christ Jesus."* 1 Timothy 2:5
2. **Jesus is the only way to the Father;** John 14:6; John 10:7, 8; 1 Timothy 2:5.
3. **There is no salvation in any other name;** Acts 4:10, 12.
4. **God has exalted Jesus above all others and requires all men to confess Him as Lord,** Philippians 2:9-11.

These truths carry great weight because they demand urgent response from all people in a way that the religions of the world do not regardless of class, race, gender, color, tongue, or nationality.

Some of the well-known religions of the world are Hindu (2000 B.C), Buddhist (560 B.C.), Islam (610 A.D.), Krishna (965 A.D.), and New Age (1960's).

Each of these religions have extremely different beliefs and focus on one or more gods, either made from material objects or crafted from some form of mystical experience which cannot be validated.

Notice how Jesus Himself imposes the priority of the "born-again" experience on a religious leader that society had identified as a representative of God. This leader came to Him with a set of questions and priorities that did not appear to have anything to do with the requirement that Jesus put forth and emphasized as more important.

John 3:1-17,"*NOW THERE was a certain man among the Pharisees named Nicodemus, a ruler (a leader, an authority) among the Jews, Who came to Jesus at night and said to Him, Rabbi, we know and are certain that You have come from God [as] a Teacher; for no one can do these signs (these wonderworks, these miracles--and produce the proofs) that You do unless God is with him.*

Jesus answered him, I assure you, most solemnly I tell you, that unless a person is born again (anew, from above), he cannot ever see (know, be acquainted with, and experience) the kingdom of God. **Notice how Jesus responded to Nicodemus.** *Nicodemus said to Him, How can a man be born when he is old? Can he enter his mother's womb again* *and be born?*

Again notice the emphatic urgency of Jesus response. *"Jesus answered, I assure you, most solemnly I tell you, unless a man is born of water and [even] the Spirit, he cannot [ever] enter the kingdom of God. What is born of [from] the flesh is flesh [of the physical is physical]; and what is born of the Spirit is spirit."*

Next, Jesus imposes on Nicodemus a reason to question his own standing with God, even though he is considered a "Teacher of Israel". *"Marvel not [do not be surprised, astonished] at My telling you, You must all be born anew (from above). The wind blows (breathes) where it wills; and though you hear its sound, yet you neither know where it comes from nor where it is going. So it is with everyone who is born of the Spirit.*

Nicodemus answered by asking, how can all this be possible? **Jesus replied, Are you the teacher of Israel, and yet do not know nor understand these things?** *[Are they strange to you? I assure you, most solemnly I tell you, we speak only of what we know [we know absolutely what we are talking about]; we have actually seen what we are testifying to [we were eyewitnesses of it]. And* **still you do not receive our testimony [you reject and refuse our evidence--that of Myself and of all those who are born of the Spirit].**

If I have told you of things that happen right here on the earth and yet none of you believes Me, how can you believe [trust Me, adhere to Me, rely on Me] if I tell you of heavenly things?"

And yet no one has ever gone up to heaven, but there is One Who has come down from heaven--the Son of Man [Himself], Who is [dwells, has His home] in heaven.

Finally, He explains the purpose of "the brazen serpent" and its relevance to Himself. *"And just as Moses lifted up the serpent in the desert [on a pole], so must [so it is necessary that] the Son of Man be lifted up [on the cross] In order that everyone who believes in Him [who cleaves to Him, trusts Him, and relies on Him] may not perish, but have eternal life and [actually] live forever!*

For God so greatly loved and dearly prized the world that He [even] gave up His only begotten (unique) Son, so that whoever believes in (trusts in, clings to, relies on) Him shall not perish (come to destruction, be lost) but have eternal (everlasting) life."

It does not matter how we rationalize this discourse between Jesus and Nicodemus, the first point clearly stated by Jesus is that unless an individual is "born again" he cannot see [understand, make sense out of, or comprehend] the Kingdom of God [heavenly things].

Clearly from Jesus' point of view, nothing in this life is to be viewed as more important than the inclusion of God and His Kingdom in our individual lives.

Although Nicodemus may have come out of his own motivations to ask Jesus questions that were important to him, Jesus wasted no time explaining the greater priority for Nicodemus and the entire world.

Jesus answered him, *"I assure you, most solemnly I tell you, that unless a person is born again [anew, from above], he cannot ever see [know, be acquainted with, and experience] the kingdom of God."*

Notice how Jesus responded to Nicodemus

concerning the necessity of the second birth.

My reason for taking this approach is because I believe that *birth is the beginning of life. However, to be born again is the beginning of a new life* with God through His Son, in His Kingdom. It is to be born from above, to a heavenly life in constant communion with God as a partaker of the divine nature.

This is clearly the first and most important stone to be laid in the foundation of our lives if we are to ever know true success and peace in this life. Our lives must begin with a relationship with God.

Clearly Jesus wasted no time in declaring how important this new birth is before anything God does **can be understood** pertaining to His Kingdom. 1 Corinthians 2:14 explains that the natural man must become a spiritual man before he is capable of receiving and understanding of such things.

"But the natural, non-spiritual man does not accept or welcome or admit into his heart the gifts and teachings and revelations of the Spirit of God, for they are folly (meaningless nonsense) to him; and he is incapable of knowing them [of progressively recognizing, understanding, and becoming better acquainted with them] because they are spiritually discerned and estimated and appreciated.

In that he *"came to Jesus by night,"* Nicodemus seemed to have come to Jesus with his own concerns which perhaps piqued his interest and made him more curious. But, Jesus without hesitation spoke first to what should have been to Nicodemus the most important discussion, *"you must be born again"*. **Here Jesus introduced the experience of "salvation" as mandatory, not just for Nicodemus but all men.**

As I stated earlier many good persons in this life have made the same mistake as Nicodemus, where religion is concerned. Because daily living in this world is demanding, with all of its cares and snares, many times a religious approach such as attending weekly sanctuary, mosque, or temple allows an individual to feel a sense of satisfaction.

Many others see so much conflict between the mainstream religious leaders that they choose to stay away from anything that hints of serving God or befriends any practice of such madness and chaos. To them this is a very wise thing to do.

Again notice how the **"god of this world"** with a small "g" is able to confuse the issue of the importance of God in their lives.

Paul the apostle stated in 2 Corinthians 4:4, *"For the god of this world has blinded the unbelievers' minds [that they should not discern the truth], preventing them from seeing the illuminating light of the GOSPEL of the glory of Christ (the Messiah), who is the Image and Likeness of God."*

William Barclay wrote, "In other words [Jesus speaking to Nicodemus] it means believe Me when I say this. I want you to listen very carefully to what I'm about to tell you here. I assure you that to be born again you've got to be willing to receive the gift that God offers. You've got to abandon every attempt to become righteous by the things that we typically do to try to earn favor with God, which is what religion seems to be all about. Instead you need to be willing to receive a free gift of grace."

John Calvin said that, "this claim that we must be born again, **reveals that there is nothing in us that is not defective.** In essence he's saying you don't need a makeover, you need a completely new birth. You've got to start all over again. It requires a totally new kind of life than the one you have now. This is a complete reorientation. It's really something you can liken to physical birth because it's an emergence from darkness into light. The point here is that being born from above is a whole new radical experience."

When Nicodemus in verse four demonstrated that such an experience was too difficult for him to comprehend, Jesus repeated and confirmed the necessity of being born again regardless of his ignorance in verse five.

*Nicodemus said to Him," **How can a man be born when he is old? Can he enter his mother's womb again and be born?** Jesus answered, I assure you, most solemnly I tell you, **unless a man is born of water and [even] the Spirit, he cannot [ever] enter the kingdom of God.***"

Again it is increasingly clear that the purpose of this point is to establish the born-again experience as the mandatory remedy required to restore relationship with God by entering into His Kingdom. Also to clarify that even those who fail to understand the mystery of the regeneration process cannot evade their obligation to have this life-changing experience. Otherwise, God will have no fellowship with sin no more than *light* does with *darkness*.

To further illustrate the importance of this change: In verse six Jesus shows that the *nature of man* is infected with sin which makes him unfit to enter into the Kingdom of God without being born again: Note, *"That which is born of the flesh is flesh."*

Matthew Henry points out "We are here told *what we are:* We are *flesh,* not only *corporeal* but *corrupt" which is a quote from* Genesis 6:3 **"and the LORD said, My Spirit shall not strive with man forever, for he is indeed flesh;** yet his days shall be one hundred and twenty years."

The soul is still a spiritual substance, but so wedded to the flesh, so captivated by the will of the flesh, so in love with the delights of the flesh, so employed in making provision for the flesh, that it is mostly called *flesh*; it is carnal. And what communion can there be between God, who is a *Spirit*, and a soul in this condition?

How did we *come to be so?* By being *born of the flesh!* It is a corruption that is bred *in the bone* with us, and therefore we cannot have a new nature, but we must be *born again.* The corrupt nature, which is *flesh*, takes rise from our *first birth*; therefore, the new nature which is *spirit* must take rise from a second birth.

Nicodemus spoke of entering again into his mother's womb, and being born; but, if he could do so, to what purpose? If he were born of his mother a hundred times that would not mend the matter; for still that *which is born of the flesh is flesh.*

A clean thing cannot be brought out of an unclean thing. He must seek for another original; he must be born of the Spirit or he cannot become spiritual. The case is, in short, this: Though man was made of body and soul, his spiritual part has such dominion over his corporeal part that God called him a **living soul** (Genesis. 2:7). However, **by indulging the appetite** of his flesh in the Garden, he ate the forbidden fruit. As a result, he prostituted the divine dominion of the soul to the tyranny of his sensual and was no longer a *living soul,* but flesh: *"Dust thou art."*

The living soul became dead and inactive. Thus in *the day* he sinned, he *surely died* and **became *earthly*. In this degenerate state, he begat a son *in his own likeness;*** he transmitted the human nature, which had been entirely deposited in his hands, thus corrupted and depraved. Corruption and sin are woven into our nature; **we are** *shapened in iniquity* which makes it necessary that the nature be changed. It is not enough to put on a new coat or a new face, but we must put on the new man. *"We* must be new creatures" end quote.

Something we may not have considered

There are two spheres or realms in this world. They are identified as the natural and the spiritual. The first birth (natural) addresses only the natural, but the second birth or born-again (spiritual) experience is *the remedy and the stabilizer for both realms.*

After we receive salvation or have the born- again experience we are said to be *"in this world but not of it."* It is an experience that aligns us with a higher concept of thought and state being. It requires a new way of managing life that must ascend higher than a religious practice or community identification.

Salvation affects our "standing state" or "position" with God immediately after we allow the Savior of the world, who gave His life as our Redeemer, to enter into our hearts.

Even though, the born-again experience is not a practice of the world, it is the one experience that all men of the world must engage. Without salvation, we cannot be in relationship with God and enter into the Kingdom of God.

My purpose for mentioning this is because many religions in the world do not represent God or the Holy Scriptures which are inspired by Him for communicating His will to all men.

According to these scriptures, God does not desire to see any perish, but that all come unto Him *"that they might have life and that more abundantly till it overflows."*

Entrance into this new life is to be viewed as the beginning of a new citizenship that impacts us in four primary areas of our lives; personally, spiritually, relationally, and positionally.

The new citizenship establishes a person into the Kingdom of God. The Kingdom of God is the supernatural realm which God reigns and is experienced by the Believer.

The way of the Kingdom is called the "narrow way" because many cannot understand its importance and some refuse to even consider it as an option for life.

It is also apparent in Scripture that every person who is saved must *"strive to enter in at the strait gate"* because it is difficult for individuals to desire to shift their operations, priorities, practices, and established mindsets to get into the Kingdom of God (or the heavenly realm which allows them to have constant fellowship with God).

Even after the new birth, life in the Kingdom still requires care, pains, difficulty, and diligence because the *"kingdom is always under assault or suffering violence"* at the hands of its many adversaries and foes.

Natural life with all of its many cares, problems, and worries, demand so much of us daily that often we are consumed with surviving from one day to the next. Notice the emphasis of Luke 13:22-28, in relation to the difficulty of entering the Kingdom.

"And *He went through the cities and villages, teaching, and journeying toward Jerusalem. Then one said to Him, "Lord, are there few who are saved?" And He said to them, "Strive to enter through the narrow gate, for many, I say to you, will seek to enter and will not be able.*

When once the Master of the house has risen up and shut the door, and you begin to stand outside and knock at the door, saying, 'Lord, Lord, open for us,' and He will answer and say to you, 'I do not know you, where you are from,' then you will begin to say, 'We ate and drank in Your presence, and You taught in our streets.' But He will say, 'I tell you I do not know you, where you are from. Depart from Me, all you workers of iniquity.'

There will be weeping and gnashing of teeth, when you see Abraham and Isaac and Jacob and all the prophets in the kingdom of God, and yourselves thrust out." *(NKJV)* **Compare this to the way that the Message Bible emphasizes the difficulty of entering the kingdom.**

"He went on teaching from town to village, village to town, but keeping on a steady course toward Jerusalem. *A bystander said, "Master, will only a few be saved?" He said, "Whether few or many is none of your business. Put your mind on your life with God.*

The way to life and God is vigorous and requires your total attention! A lot of people will assume that they'll sit down to God's salvation banquet **just because they've been hanging around the**

neighborhood church all their lives. Well, one day you're going to be banging on the door, wanting to get in, but you'll find the door locked and the Master saying, "Sorry, you're not on my guest list."

You'll protest, "But we've known you all our lives!" only to be interrupted with His abrupt, **"Your kind of 'knowing' is hardly knowing. You don't know the first thing about me."**

That's when you'll find yourselves out in the cold, **strangers to grace.** You'll watch Abraham, Isaac, Jacob, and all the prophets march into God's kingdom. You'll watch outsiders stream in from the east, west, north, and south and sit down at the table of God's kingdom. And all the time you'll be outside looking in—and wondering what happened. This is the Great Reversal: the last in line put at the head of the line, and the so-called first ending up last.

The reason many persons will come short of the grace of God for entering the Kingdom is because they *half-heartedly seek* that which requires a *whole- hearted commitment* and cannot be attained without diligent striving, a strong conviction, and a determined resolve to press forward trusting God every step of the way.

Here it is clear in the words of Jesus that a day will come, where in a "door of distinction" will be shut and those left standing in the outer court will be kept out. Even though, the door of mercy and grace has been left open a long time so that anyone could enter, it will be that the master Himself will rise up and shut the door to "separate the sheep from the goat." "The sinners will no longer be able to stand in the congregation of the righteous."

Some may have hoped to enter in using their own measures but the lesson of Noah teaches that God will shut the door and exclude everyone who refused to heed His voice during the hour of their visitations.

What makes this important!

I'm pressed to appeal to you who strive to achieve and accomplish in this life, because I know how difficult it is to juggle your personal success with submission to God. Especially, since we may have already accomplished a great deal without having a personal relationship with Him.

We may even be responsible for many of the significant things that Believers and non-believers are privileged to enjoy daily; but fail to appreciate because the recipients don't understand the impact of our works upon the infrastructure of our society.

But the fact is, we can achieve much more with the accommodation of God's grace than we've ever imagined. I always say it this way; "Those who are great accomplishers and achievers using their gifts and talents without Christ have not even scratched the surface of their God given ability to succeed *until like branches, they are connected to* [Christ] *the true vine."*

Matter-of-fact, we were not only created to succeed, but we were created to also glorify God in the process of becoming successful. That way, others might have hope in this life when they watch the hand of God move for us. This type of success is called *true success* and results in peace and wholesomeness because Heaven backs it.

I've practiced as a successful professional artist for more than thirty years and have been challenged in ways that would frustrate the place of God in my life because of the many privileges and opportunities the profession gives me.

But nothing is as precious as knowing who I am and my true purpose in the sight of God, who gave my life balance and symmetry at all times. He directs me by the spirit of His Word.

The Psalmist wrote a very befitting verse, "Some folk would rather have houses and land, some folk chose silver and gold. But these things they treasure and *forget about their Soul.* I've decided to make Jesus my choice."

Friend, God's problem with us is neither our stuff or our success; it is that we may have forgotten to include Him as **the most important ingredient** and "securer of our souls." **Don't be like the people of the Samaritan Village who rejected the Savior.**

Now it came to pass, when the time had come for Him to be received up, that He steadfastly set His face to go to Jerusalem, and sent messengers before His face. And as they went, they entered a village of the Samaritans, to prepare for Him. **But they did not receive Him,** *because His face was set for the journey to Jerusalem. And when His disciples James and John saw this, they said, "Lord, do You want us to command fire to come down from heaven and consume them, just as Elijah did?"*

But He turned and rebuked them, and said, *"You do not know what manner of spirit you are of. For the Son of Man did not come to destroy men's lives but to save them."* **And they went to another village.** Luke 9:51-56 (NKJV)

Don't allow religious practices, worldly status, authority over others, nor hypocrisy to cause you to fail to receive the Savior. Luke 11:37-54

And as He spoke, a certain Pharisee [religious] asked Him to dine with him. So He went in and sat down to eat. **When the Pharisee saw it,** *he marveled that He had not first washed before dinner.*

Then the Lord said to him, "Now you Pharisees **make the outside of the cup and dish clean,** *but your inward part is full of greed and wickedness. Foolish ones! Did not He who made the outside make the inside also? But rather give alms of such things as you have; then indeed all things are clean to you.*

"But, woe to you Pharisees! For **you tithe** *mint and rue and all manner of herbs, and pass by justice and the love of God. These you ought to have done, without leaving the others undone. Woe to you Pharisees! For you* **love the best seats** *in the synagogues and greetings in the marketplaces. Woe to you, scribes and Pharisees, hypocrites! For you are* **like graves which are not seen,** *and the men who walk over them are not aware of them."*

Then one of the **lawyers [status]** *answered and said to Him, "Teacher, by saying these things You reproach us also." And He said, "Woe to you also, lawyers! For* **you load men with burdens hard to bear, and you yourselves do not touch the burdens with one of your fingers.** *Woe to you! For you build the tombs of the prophets, and your fathers killed them.*

In fact, you bear witness that you approve the deeds of your fathers; for they indeed killed them, and you build their tombs. Therefore the wisdom of God also said, I will send them prophets and apostles, and some of them they will kill and persecute, that the blood of all the prophets which was shed from the foundation of the world may be required of this generation, from the blood of Abel to the blood of Zechariah who perished between the altar and the temple. Yes, I say to you, it shall be required of this generation.

"Woe to you lawyers [authority]! **For you have taken away the key of knowledge. You did not enter in yourselves, and those who were entering in you hindered."**

And as He said these things to them, the scribes and the Pharisees began to assail Him vehemently, and to cross-examine Him about many things, lying in wait for Him, and seeking to catch Him in something He might say, that they might accuse Him. [Hypocrisy]

I submit that Satan has used Religion along with many worldly lusts to deceive many, blinding their minds from the truth and corrupting souls with many divisive and deceitful evils.

As I continue this discussion I want to represent godly success from a scriptural perspective in a way that helps to clear up God's purpose and plan for our peace and prosperity.

The Bible addresses two specific areas related to Jesus Christ the Son of God as He lived as the son of man in the earth realm. The areas are: 1) the **person** of Christ and 2) the **principles** on which He based His entire operation. They are called "Kingdom Principles."

We receive the person of Christ into our hearts at the moment of our salvation and are immediately redeemed from the curse of the law; we are adopted as children of God, and are freed from eternal damnation. Even though our sonship in the Kingdom of God comes through the regenerating of the Holy Spirit, we are made better in this new life progressively by the aid of the Holy Spirit as we submit daily to renewing our minds to His [God's] will (Romans 12:1-2).

This submission to Kingdom Principles is referred to as *"working out your own salvation or laboring to enter into His rest."* From these spiritually adopted methods, we who are Kingdom citizens are to achieve success in a way that glorifies God and does not offend the premise of who we were created to be.

On another note, let me submit to you that there is simply no way possible for a man to obey the Scriptures and **fail to achieve** prosperity. In Paul's admonition to Timothy, he advised him to *"Meditate upon these things; give thyself wholly to them; that **thy profiting may appear to all.** Take heed unto thyself, and unto the doctrine; continue in them: for in doing this thou shalt both save thyself, and them that hear thee."*

CHAPTER

2

WORKING OUT YOUR SALVATION

(1 Timothy 4:15, 16)

We have been given power to live as a son of God by the aid of the Holy-Spirit, but we must take the responsibility of renewing our minds and obeying all that is revealed

*"For I am not ashamed of the **Gospel** (good news) of Christ, for it is **God's power working unto salvation** [for deliverance from eternal death] to everyone who believes with a personal trust and a confident surrender and firm reliance, to the Jew first and also to the Greek, For **in the Gospel a righteousness** which God ascribes is **revealed**, both springing from faith and leading to faith [disclosed through the way of faith that arouses to more faith]. As it is written, the man who through faith is just and upright shall live and shall live by faith (Romans 1:16, 17).*

*"Therefore, my dear ones, as you have always obeyed [my suggestions], so now, not only [with the enthusiasm you would show] in my presence but much more because I am absent, work out (**cultivate,***

carry out to the goal, and fully complete) your own salvation with reverence and awe and trembling (self-distrust, with serious caution, tenderness of conscience, watchfulness against temptation, timidly shrinking from whatever might offend God and discredit the name of Christ)." (Philippians 2:12)

"How shall we escape [appropriate retribution] if we neglect and refuse to pay attention to such a great salvation [as is now offered to us, letting it drift past us forever]? For it was declared at first by the Lord [Himself], and it was confirmed to us and proved to be real and genuine by those who personally heard Him speak (Hebrews 2:3).

Now that we have it we must work it out! These three references combined illustrate the fact that salvation comes with a great responsibility for all new converts. Clearly it is not that God has given us a new life through the second birth to become idle and consumed with our own selfish agenda. There is a daily demand for self-denial, preoccupancy with cross bearing, and following or imitating Jesus.

To "deny yourself" without taking up the cross is simply not enough. This only submits an individual to a new life that grows non-progressive, idle, and boring because its purpose is distorted. Throughout the years of my life, I noticed one truth consistently taught across all denominations is the need to be born again. The failure of the church has certainly not been a lack of opportunities for salvation because in many Sunday morning services around the U.S. and around the world the entire focus is on getting as many persons saved as possible.

What to do with salvation or the new life, how it will manifest, or how to work it out after one receives it is the missing link that has cost many converts the privileges of "the born-again" experience. This also confuses the Believer of his or her importance in systems and processes that are responsible for governing our world.

How can we work out a salvation of which we are ignorant? Why ask religious questions that require no confirmable Scriptural answers? Or, why continue to embrace the expressions of unlearned participants who answer in ways which suggest that "the will of God is responsible for the good and evil things that are happening in their lives"?

Failure to read, study the Bible, pray, and meditate on the Scriptures, confess and believe God's Word as the primary source of the new life has left many in derision about how to subdue simple challenges of the new life.

If it's true that approximately five percent of all Christians read their Bibles daily, I submit that a great deal of confusion has set in the church and in the minds of people as a result of this neglect.

Working out our salvation requires getting to know the will of God by consistently hearing the Word of God preached for the development of our faith; learning to discern the voice of the Holy Spirit; studying His Word; approaching every situation or circumstance with prayer; and obeying God's commands with as much specificity as humanly possible.

The consistent practice of these things is considered "Spiritual labors" that enable the Believer to grow strong in faith and trust in God. Notice how the Apostle Paul addressed the Thessalonians regarding this issue:

*"Finally then, brethren, we urge and exhort in the Lord Jesus that you should **abound more and more**, just as you received from us how you ought to walk and to please God; for you know what commandments we gave you through the Lord Jesus. **For this is the will of God**, your sanctification: that you should abstain from sexual immorality; that each of you should **know how to possess his own vessel in sanctification and honor,** not in passion of lust, like the Gentiles who do not know God; that no one should take advantage of and defraud his brother in this matter, because the Lord is the avenger of all such, as we also forewarned you and testified. For God did not call us to uncleanness, but in holiness. Therefore he who rejects this does not reject man, but God, who has also given us His Holy Spirit."* (1 Thessalonians 4:1-10, *NKJV*)

These **spiritual laborers** are the means that empower the Believer to enter into God's promised rest.

LABORING TO ENTER INTO HIS REST

We must live according to the will of God which requires knowing His revealed will. I've listed several references to establish this point, starting with the time when Jesus was actually tested in the wilderness by Satan. He quoted from the words of Moses in Deuteronomy 8:3, "But He answered and said, "It is written, *'Man shall not live by bread alone, but **by every word that proceeds from the mouth of God."*** (Matthew 4:4).

In the gospel of John 5:30, He made it clear that apart from the will of God He had no will of His own. Note, *"I can of Myself do nothing. As I hear, I judge; and My judgment is righteous, because I do not seek My own will but **the will of the Father** who sent Me."*

Hebrew 4:10-11, *"For he who has entered His rest has himself also ceased **from his works** as God did from His. Let us therefore be diligent to enter that rest, lest anyone fall according to the same example of disobedience. For **the word of God is living and powerful,** and sharper than any two-edged sword, piercing even to the division of soul and spirit, and of joints and marrow, and is a discerner of the thoughts and intents of the heart."*

A divine Key:
There are "secret things and revealed things"

Deuteronomy 29:29, "The **secret things** belong unto the Lord our God, but the **things which are revealed belong to us and to our children forever,** *that we may do all of the words of this law."* (AMP)

Notice how the Message Bible says it; *"GOD, our God, will take care of the hidden things **but the revealed things are our business.** It's up to us and our children **to attend to all the terms in this Revelation."***

Romans 11:33, *"How unsearchable are God's judgments, and his ways past finding out!"* I use these passages to illustrate verse twenty-nine, secret things belong to the Lord our God.

What makes this an important Key?

First, the Word of God forbids our curious minds inquiring into the secret counsels of God and making determinations concerning them. It is God's prerogative that we spend our time with what is revealed or "the revealed will of God." There are questions which cannot be answered and therefore are not to be asked. **They are matters of God's sovereign, secret will.** It is also presumptuous for us to pry into the—*the mysteries of government*, and to inquire into the reasons of state which *it is not for us to know* unless it becomes our personal duty or positional responsibility. See Acts 1:7, *"And He said to them, "It is **not for you to know** times or seasons which the Father has put in His own authority."*

Secondly, We are directed and encouraged to diligently inquire into those things which God has made known: "things *revealed belong to us and to our children .*" (Deuteronomy 29:29)

1. Though God has kept much of his counsel secret, there is enough revealed to satisfy and thoroughly save us. He has kept back nothing that is profitable for us but only that which is good for us to be ignorant.

2. We ought to acquaint ourselves and our children with the things of God that have been revealed. They are the rules we live by; the principles we build our lives upon; and therefore we must learn them ourselves; and teach them diligently to our children.

3. All our knowledge must be for the sake of practice and application. This is the aim of all divine revelation, not to entertain us but to furnish us with useful information that can assist us in times of need.

*"But **be doers of the word**, and not hearers only, deceiving yourselves. For if anyone is a hearer of the word and not a doer, he is like a man observing his natural face in a mirror; for he observes himself, goes away, and immediately forgets what kind of man he was. But he who looks into the perfect law of liberty and continues in it, and is **not a forgetful hearer but a doer of the work, this one will be blessed in what he does."** (James 1:23-25)*

FAITH BEGINS WHERE THE WILL OF GOD IS KNOWN

Again, Jesus made it clear *"I am able to do nothing from Myself* [independently, of My own accord--but only as I am taught by God and as I get His orders]. *Even as I hear, I judge* [**I decide as I am bidden** to decide. **As the voice comes to Me,** so I give a decision], *and My judgment is right* (just, righteous), *because **I do not seek or consult My own will*** [I have no desire to do what is pleasing to Myself, My own aim, My own purpose] *but **only the will and pleasure of the Father*** *Who sent Me.* (John 5:30, AMP)

Our Kingdom citizenship must not be experienced by guessing and assuming, we are called to know the truth so that we can freely live as children of God who daily walk and live by faith. Faith, which is the substance, evidence, and currency of Heaven, has three distinct parts; knowledge, assent, and appropriation.

Knowledge in this usage is to "know" as Jesus stated *"I am able to do nothing from Myself* [independently of My own accord--but **only**

as I am taught by God and as I get His orders].

Assent is agreement which must be clear that *knowing* and *agreeing* with God's Word does not equal faith. It is only "belief" which may only exist in one's mind without demanding a response or action. We know and agree with many things that never challenge us to act. Even *"The devils believe and tremble."* (James 2:19)

Appropriation means to make something one's own, or to take for one's own exclusive or specific use. Here "faith" is established when we are willing to appropriate [act on] what we **know** and **assent** [agree] with that God or His Word has revealed to us.

So the reason I say that "faith begins where the will of God is known is because until we are clear and definitive about what God promises or expects from us, we have no distinct place to begin holding God accountable to His Word nor do we have the right to expect God to meet our expectations.

This is the primary reason Paul speaks of the urgency of mind renewal for all converts in Romans 12:2, so we understand the three phases of God's will.

"I APPEAL to you therefore, brethren, and beg of you in view of [all] the mercies of God, to make a decisive dedication of your bodies [presenting all your members and faculties] *as a living sacrifice, holy* (devoted, consecrated) *and well pleasing to God, which is your reasonable* (rational, intelligent) *service and spiritual worship.*

Do not be conformed to this world (this age), [fashioned after and adapted to its external, superficial customs], *but be transformed* **(changed)** *by the* [entire] *renewal of your mind* [by its new ideals and its new attitude], *so that you may prove* [for yourselves] *what is the good and acceptable and perfect will of God, even the thing which is good and acceptable and perfect* [in His sight for you].

Ephesians 1:9-12 further ratifies the importance of the revealed will of God, *"Making known to us the mystery* (secret) *of His will* (of His plan, of His purpose). [And it is this:] *In accordance with His good pleasure* (His merciful intention) *which He had previously purposed and set forth in Him, [He planned] for the maturity of the times and the climax of the ages to unify all things and head them up and consummate them in Christ, [both] things in heaven and things on the earth.*

In Him we also were made [God's] *heritage (portion) and we obtained an inheritance; for we had been foreordained (chosen and appointed beforehand) in accordance with His purpose,* **Who works out everything in agreement with the counsel and design of His [own] will,**

So that we who first hoped in Christ [who first put our confidence in Him have been destined and appointed to] live for the praise of His glory! 1 John 2:17 "And the world passes away and disappears, and with it the forbidden cravings (the passionate desires, the lust) of it; **but he who does the will of God and carries out His purposes in his life abides (remains) forever.**

In teaching His disciples to pray, Jesus taught them to practice the rudiment of saying, "Your kingdom come, Your will be done on earth as it is in heaven," (Matthew 6:10)

John 15:4-7, *Dwell in Me, and I will dwell in you. [Live in Me, and I will live in you.] Just as no branch can bear fruit of itself without abiding in (being vitally united to) the vine, neither can you bear fruit unless you abide in Me. I am the Vine; you are the branches. Whoever lives in Me and I in him bears much (abundant) fruit. However, apart from Me [cut off from vital union with Me] you can do nothing.*

*If a person does not dwell in Me, he is thrown out like a [broken-off] branch, and withers; such branches are gathered up and thrown into the fire, and they are burned. If you live in Me [abide vitally united to Me] and **My words** remain in you and continue to live in your hearts, **ask whatever you will, and it shall be done for you.***

*1 John 5:14-17, And this is the confidence (the assurance, the privilege of boldness) which we have in Him: [we are sure] **that if we ask anything** (make any request) **according to His will (in agreement with His own plan),** He listens to and hears us. And if (since) we [positively] know that He listens to us in whatever we ask, we also know [with settled and absolute knowledge] that we have [granted us as our present possessions] the requests made of Him.*

THE WILL OF GOD IS NOT AUTOMATIC

Contrary to popular opinion, many presume that the will of God is automatic because God is sovereign. The Scriptures actually teach that God has given the earth into the hands of men. This also means that our success will be determined by us, not God. Without knowledge of the will of God we set ourselves up for many heartbreaks and failures that can be avoided through understanding how salvation works.

PROBLEMS ASSOCIATED WITH SALVATION (SOTERIA)

is

The lack of **ORIENTATION and TRAINING** results in **DENIED MANIFESTATION** because of **WRONG APPLICATIONS** and a **NEW SPIRITUAL LIFE** without **CONFIRMATION**

Problems arise to interfere with the implementation of successful salvation when Kingdom citizens are passive, procrastinators, and prideful:

When we are **PASSIVE** we are submissive to our fleshly, carnal reasoning points of views, logics, and ways without demanding change from ourselves. Change begins with self honesty and a commitment to fix what is broken or not working in our lives regardless of whether others are aware of it or not. Notice Romans 12:1-2, *"I beseech you therefore, brethren, by the mercies of God, that you **present your bodies** a living sacrifice, holy, acceptable to God, which is your reasonable service. And **do not be conformed** to this world, **but be transformed** by the renewing of your mind, that you may prove what is that good and acceptable and perfect will of God."*

When we **procrastinate** we become wasteful of the opportunities to please God as we are slow to upgrade the quality of our new life and relationships. Joshua 1:8 and John 8:31-32 make this point very clear.

"This Book of the Law shall not depart from your mouth, but you shall meditate in it day and night, that you may observe to do according

to all that is written in it. For then you will make your way prosperous, and then you will have good success."

"Then Jesus said to those Jews who believed Him, "If you abide in My word, you are My disciples indeed. And you shall know the truth, and the truth shall make you free."

When we are **prideful,** we deceive ourselves and allow others to think we are something that we are not; rather than putting forth the effort necessary to become someone better than they can imagine. Here, self honesty and a sincere commitment to obey the small intricate details in the Scriptures, which will keep us from error.

Let us be careful not to base our determination to live a godly life on what religious people are doing and their methods of discriminating against certain Scriptural truths which seem too difficult to adhere to. We cannot live in offense with any Scriptural justification nor can we expect God to be blind to any of our hypocrisies, hidden schemes, ethical violations, or moral failures.

I have learned that it is best to do righteousness from an upright position, or our operation will cease to be Holy. When it fails to be Holy or in strict compliance with the Scriptures, we will not experience the depth of God's favor.

But if we are able to *"endure hardness as a good soldier"* during the process, we may feel isolated and forsaken but after the trial has ceased we'll have great reason to rejoice.

There are a multitude of God- fearing Christians and good people all over this world who fall short of experiencing God's best. They are simply out of step with their destiny because of a lack of conformity to, and a misappropriation of, Proverbs 18:13, Prov. 26:17, Matthew 18, Galatians 6, and Ephesians 5, 6.

Here is an interesting plea for wisdom written in Proverbs 1:12-33 that I believe every reader should cautiously observe. At certain times in our lives, it is simply necessary to re-evaluate our practices to ensure we have not strayed from right paths and practices.

Notice, *"Lady Wisdom goes out in the street and shouts. At the town center she makes her speech. In the middle of the traffic she takes her stand. At the busiest corner she calls out: "Simpletons! How long will we wallow in ignorance?*

Cynics! How long will you feed your cynicism? Idiots! How long will you refuse to learn? About face! I can revise your life. Look, I'm ready to pour out my spirit on you;

I'm ready to tell you all I know. As it is, I've called, but you've turned a deaf ear; I've reached out to you, but you've ignored me. "Since you laugh at my counsel and make a joke of my advice, How can I take you seriously? I'll turn the tables and joke about your troubles!

What if the roof falls in and your whole life goes to pieces? What if catastrophe strikes and there's nothing to show for your life but rubble and ashes? You'll need me then. You'll call for me but don't expect an answer. No matter how hard you look, you won't find me.

"Because you hated Knowledge and had nothing to do with the Fear-of-God, Because you wouldn't take my advice and brushed aside all my offers to train you. Well, you've made your bed—now lie in it; you wanted your own way—now, how do you like it? Don't you see what happens, you simpletons, you idiots? Carelessness kills; complacency

is murder. First pay attention to me, and then relax.

Now you can take it easy—you're in good hands." (Message)

Let's review Hosea 4:6, *My people are destroyed for lack of knowledge. Because you have rejected knowledge, I also will reject you from being priest for Me; because you have forgotten the law of your God, I also will forget your children.*

Also Hebrews 3:10-14 states, "Therefore I was angry with that generation, And said, they always go astray *in their heart,* **and they have not known My ways.** So I swore in My wrath, they shall not enter My rest. Beware, brethren, lest there be in any of you **an evil heart of unbelief** in departing from the living God; but exhort one another daily, while it is called "Today," lest any of you [us] be hardened through the deceitfulness of sin. For we have become partakers of Christ if we hold the beginning of our confidence steadfast to the end.

Each of these passages make it clear that the enjoyment of the new life will be severely crippled by our old ways of functioning and operating; if we allow passivity, pride, or procrastination to exist in our pursuit of Godliness and righteousness.

Soteria: The Privileges of Salvation

WE ARE REDEEMED BACK TO THE STATE OF MAN BEFORE THE FALL OF GENESIS THREE WHICH CENTERS OUR NEW LIFE ON TWO PRIORITIES

They are the **Presence of God and the Voice of God.** The

presence of God "garden of Eden" means "delight." The **voice** of God means "leading or being lead." Together they imply that as we delight ourselves in the presence of God and the Word of God, He will direct us by speaking to us about life and its many issues.

We must understand that before sin entered the world by the disobedience of Adam, fellowship with God was the norm. Adam operated as a son of God. After sin entered into the world Adam and Eve were put out of the Garden of Eden and translated into the kingdom of darkness which resulted in a loss of identity and purpose.

Satan's ability to deceive them cost all humanity (the seed of Adam) the birth privilege of "Son-ship" in the Kingdom of God.

Here We Receive our Introduction to the Real Privileges of the Second Birth

The power of the second birth

The born- again experience put us back into the Kingdom of God which means we have access by the blood of Jesus, to God as our Father and the many privileges of adoption as sons.

To appropriately address the born-again experience, it requires an understanding of **"The Death of Jesus Christ" and how it confirms the covenant promises** listed throughout the Scriptures. I found this to be an effective way to prove God's intention for healing, miracles, and prosperity. It also clarifies the need to walk in constant self-denial.

If we attempt to eliminate the doctrine of the death of Christ from the salvation experience, it would mean the surrender of a unique, God-mandated experience for men to regain right standing with God.

Many have stated, "it is the redemption feature that distinguishes Christianity from other religions." If we surrender this distinctive, Christian doctrine from its creed, then this supreme experience is **brought to the level of other religions.**

Other great men have been valued for their lives; Christ, above all others, has been valued for His death, where both God and man were reconciled.

The Cross is recognized as "the vertical and horizontal magnet which sends the electric current between Earth and Heaven, and it makes the inclusion of God through the death of His Son a saving truth." This is a truth that is consistently ratified throughout the Scriptures.

Jesus Christ partook of flesh and blood in order that He might die (Hebrews 2:14). According to (1 John 3:5) *"He was manifested to take away our sins."* Christ came into this world to give His life as a ransom for many (Matthews 20:28). **The purpose** of the coming of Christ into the world and because He assumed a nature like our own, He was able offer up His life as the perfect sacrifice for the sins of men.

In my book, *Understanding Your Salvation,* I explain what happened at the death of Christ and the immediate impact it has on all of us who conceive the four primary things that was accomplished when He said "It is finished." As we grasp the significant power of the knowledge of His death and resurrection, we begin to gain by faith how we are raised in the newness of life.

The Scriptures set forth the death of Jesus Christ in a four-fold way. This way describes Jesus as 1) our ransom, 2) our propitiation, 3) our reconciliation, and 4) our substitution.

The meaning of a **ransom** is clearly set forth in Leviticus 25:47-49, which means to deliver a thing or person by paying a price; to buy back a person or thing by paying the price for which it is held in captivity. Christ redeemed us from the curse of a broken law by Himself being made a curse for us. His death was the ransom price paid for our deliverance.

Christ is the **propitiation** for our sins; He is set forth by God as a **propitiation** through His blood. Propitiation means mercy-seat, or covering. The mercy-seat covering the Ark of the Covenant was called **propitiation** (Exodus 25:22; Hebrews 9:5). It is that by which God covers, overlooks, and pardons the penitent and believing sinner because of Christ's death. **Propitiation** furnishes a ground on the basis of which God could set forth His righteousness and yet pardon sinful men (Romans 3:25, 26; Hebrews 9:15). We are reconciled to God by the death of His Son, by His Cross, and by the blood of His Cross--that is the message of these Scriptures.

Reconciliation has two sides; active and passive. In the active sense we may look upon Christ's death as removing the enmity existing between God and man and which had hitherto been a barrier to fellowship (see the above quoted texts). This state of existing enmity is set forth in such Scriptures as Romans 8:7, "Because the carnal mind is enmity against God." Additional Scriptures include Ephesians 2:15 and James 4:4. In the passive sense of the word it may indicate the change of attitude on the part of man toward God, this change being wrought in the heart of man by a vision of the Cross of Christ; a change from enmity to friendship thus taking place. (2 Corinthians 5:20)

The story of the Passover Lamb (Exodus 12), with 1 Corinthians 5:7, illustrates the meaning of **substitution:** one life given in the stead of another. "The Lord hath laid on him the iniquity of us all." God made Christ, who knew no sin, to be sin for us. Christ Himself bore our sins in His own body on the tree ..." this is **substitution.** Christ died in our place, bore our sins, paid the penalty due for our sins, and all this, not by force, but willingly (John 10:17, 18).

To further clarify, notice how in Jesus' conversation with the two disciples on the way to Emmaus, He claimed that Moses, all the prophets, and all the Scriptures dealt with the subject of His death. (Luke 24:27, 44)

"Then beginning with Moses and [throughout] all the Prophets, He went on explaining and interpreting to them in all the Scriptures the things concerning and referring to Himself.

44Then He said to them, this is what I told you while I was still with you: everything which is written concerning Me in the Law of Moses and the Prophets and the Psalms must be fulfilled."

Also Peter claimed that the death of Christ was the one great subject into which the Old Testament prophets searched deeply (1 Peter 1:11, 12). Notice, *"They sought [to find out] to whom or when this was to come which the Spirit of Christ working within them was indicating when He predicted the sufferings of Christ and the glories that should follow [them]. It was then disclosed to them that the services they were rendering were not meant for themselves and their period of time, but for you. [It is these very] things which have now already been made known plainly to you by those who preached the good news (the Gospel) to you by the [same] Holy Spirit sent from heaven. Into these things [the very] angels long to look!"*

One out of every forty-four verses of Scripture in the New Testament deals with this theme, and **the death of Christ is mentioned 175 times.**

It must also be considered **the foundational theme of the gospel** acknowledging that Paul said: *"I delivered unto you first of all* [i.e., first in order; the first plank in the Gospel platform; the truth of primary importance] *. . . that **Christ died for our sins"*** (1 Corinthians 15:1-3). There can be no gospel story, message, or preaching without the chronicle of the death of Christ as the Redeemer of men.

One of the most difficult truths for Believers to conceive after salvation is that the miraculous gifts of **healing and prosperity** (progressive salvation) *are as much a part of the process of salvation* as are all the other promises listed in Scriptures.

For instance, 3 John 1:2, clearly states, *"Beloved, I pray that you may **prosper** in all things and be in **health**, just as your soul prospers."* And, 1 Peter 2:24, states, *"who **Himself bore** our **sins** in His own body on the tree, **that we, having died to sins**, might live for righteousness— **by whose stripes you were healed."***

But to grasp the "healing" conferred to, the new convert through salvation requires three things;

1. Total heart trust and confidence in the Lord.

2. Surrendering your former understanding.

3. Dependence and reliance on the finished work of Christ. Read Proverbs 3:5-8 along with Romans 6:1-3 in the Amplified Bible.

"Lean on, trust in, and be confident in the Lord with all your heart and mind and do not rely on your own insight or understanding. In all your ways know, recognize, and acknowledge Him and He will direct and make straight and plain your paths. Be not wise in your own eyes; reverently fear and worship the Lord and turn [entirely] away from evil. It shall be health to your nerves and sinews, and marrow and moistening to your bones."

*"Are you ignorant of the fact that all of us who have been baptized into Christ Jesus were baptized into His death? We were buried therefore with Him by the baptism into death, so that just as Christ was raised from the dead by the glorious [power] of the Father, so we too might [habitually] live and behave in newness of life. For **if we have become one with Him by sharing a death** like His, **we shall also be [one with Him in sharing] His resurrection** [by a new life lived for God]."*

I will not discuss these issues just for the sake of discussion or to prove some mute intellectual point that merits no life-change. My intent is to assist Kingdom citizens in grasping the benefits associated with covenant relationship through the salvation experience.

To clarify the importance of a Believers' need to understand how we inherit the method God used to secure deliverance and healing for us. The Bible thoroughly discusses what happened at the death of Christ and the immediate impact it has on the *"believing"* recipients of this great salvation.

THE TRUTH IS
All may Prosper and be Healed

Isaiah 53: 4-5, the Amplified Bible, states that "*Surely He has borne "our" grief's [sicknesses, weaknesses, and distresses] and **carried "our"** sorrows and pains [of punishment], **yet "we" [ignorantly] considered Him** stricken, smitten, and afflicted by God [as if with leprosy]. But **He was wounded for** "our" transgressions, He was **bruised for** "our" guilt and iniquities; the **chastisement** [needful to obtain] peace and well-being for "us" was upon Him, and **with the stripes** [that wounded] Him "we" are **healed and made whole. Clearly the implications are for all of us who "believe."***

Next notice the emphasis of **Matthew 8: 15-17,** "*He touched her hand and the fever left her; and she got up and began waiting on Him. When evening came, **they brought to Him "many" who were under the power of demons,** and He drove out the spirits with a word **and restored to health "all" who were sick.** And thus He fulfilled what was spoken by the prophet Isaiah, **He Himself took** [in order to carry away] **our weaknesses and infirmities and bore away "our" diseases.***"

Also observe, **Matthews 9: 35** "*And Jesus went about all the cities and villages, teaching in their synagogues and proclaiming the good news [the Gospel] of the kingdom and "curing **all kinds** of disease and **every** weakness and infirmity.*"

Clearly our crisis in manifestation is a crisis in "Belief".

Luke 6: 17-19, *"And Jesus came down with them and took His stand on a level spot, with a great crowd of His disciples and a vast throng of people from all over Judea and Jerusalem and the seacoast of Tyre and Sidon, who came to listen to Him and* **to be cured of their diseases- - Even those who were disturbed and troubled with unclean spirits, and they were being healed [also].**

And all the multitude was seeking to touch Him, for healing power was all the while going forth from Him and or calamities. **[curing them all and saving them from severe illnesses]**

Hebrews 8:6, *"But as it now is, He [Christ] has acquired a [priestly] ministry which is as much superior and more excellent [than the old] as the covenant (the agreement) of which He is the Mediator [the Arbiter, Agent] is superior and more excellent, [because] it is enacted and rests upon more important [sublimer, higher, and nobler] promises.*

Matthew 15:22-28 says *"Jesus was touched by the faith of the Canaanite woman. Notice, And behold, a woman who was a Canaanite from that district came out and, with a [loud, troublesomely urgent] cry, begged, have mercy on me, O Lord, Son of David! My daughter is miserably and distressingly and cruelly possessed by a demon!*

But He did not answer her a word. And His disciples came and implored Him, saying; Send her away, for she is crying out after us. He answered, I was sent only to the lost sheep of the house of Israel. But she came and, kneeling, worshiped Him and kept praying, Lord, help me! And He answered, It is not right (proper, becoming, or fair) to take the children's bread and throw it to the little dogs. **She said, Yes, Lord, yet** *even the little pups (little whelps) eat the crumbs that fall from their [young] masters' table. Then Jesus answered her, O woman, great is your faith! Be it done for you as you wish. **And her daughter was cured from that moment".***

Also notice the emphasis of James 5:13-20, ***"Is "anyone" among you suffering?*** *Let him pray. Is anyone cheerful? Let him sing psalms. Is **"anyone"** among you sick? Let him call for the elders of the church, and let them pray over him, anointing him with oil in the name of the Lord. And **the prayer of faith** will save the sick, and the Lord will raise him up. And if he has committed sins, he will be forgiven.*

*Confess your trespasses to one another, and **pray for one another, that you may be healed.** The effective, fervent prayer of a righteous man avails much. Elijah was a man with a nature like ours, and he prayed earnestly that it would not rain; and it did not rain on the land for three years and six months. And he prayed again, and the heaven gave rain, and the earth produced its fruit. "*

Many other infallible proofs declare that it is God's will that all Believers are healed. But, Mark 9:23 emphasize the fact that there must be "belief" in the substance of faith in order for the possibility of God's miracle power to be made manifest.

CHAPTER
3

SOCIAL MALPRACTICE

Each day I see so much waste because of misdirected energy, unclear roles, misappropriated assignments, and wrong pieces being forced to conform where they are not designed to fit. Many educational institutions are often consumed with achieving academic excellence and scholastic achievement that they fail to tailor programs to fit individual needs.

My conviction is that each student be catered to according their uniqueness, individual gifts, and personal skills, which in my view are their primary needs.

However, it appears that our society is beginning to realize that everyone is not designed to be an educational expert. For years this confusion of focus has distorted the mission of our world causing overcrowding and under achievement by proportions never intended by our Creator.

More of today's educational methods that are systematically

determined must result from extensive assessments and evaluations of each child's personal interest during their early and most critical learning years. Then, we must administer the unique education and training model that corresponds to the child's personal needs. If we take this approach, the nation would witness a drastic decline in dropout rates, drug-abuse, crime, violence, teen-pregnancy, single-parent families, and many other hindrances within our communities. I'm not suggesting it would solve all of our social problems, but I am confident it will have a positive impact. Simply put, children would be less stressed and frustrated due to a lack of personal motivation and unforced participation.

Additionally, it would promote increased focus, stimulated interest, and a passionate desire in learning institutions. I say this because I almost drowned in the system under the radar due to a variety of undetected problems during my elementary and middle school years. Even though, I tried very hard initially, it felt like doors were closing rapidly from every side. I shut myself in and through misdirected pride, I kept others out. Even those in positions to help were not allowed to assist me.

I remember vividly the frustrations I kept vaulted inside that swiftly became my fear of not being able to cope. I was not able to understand academics like my siblings, relatives, or classmates. Afraid of letting my parents down, I was intimidated by the scholastic achievements of my elder sister and embarrassed by the accelerated accomplishments of my younger brother. This, for me, was a real trap.

I remember when relatives and neighborhood families would come together during report card time to proudly share the grades of their children. I never looked forward to those times. For a while I seemed only able to consistently earn an "A" in conduct. My parents were hard working and very caring; always busy creating opportunities for us. My siblings were smart and my family and friends were very caring. Yet, I perceived this network of support as pressure to do better. But it seemed that the harder I tried, the more difficult it became to comprehend the classroom lessons.

One day, I remember sitting at the dining table approximately forty-five minutes to an hour trying to solve one math problem so I could play basketball. Back then, we were not allowed to do anything after school until our homework and house chores were completed. My younger brother walked in, looked over my shoulder, and pointed his finger at the page and said, "This is simple bro. Change this, move that over, erase the way you started off, and that's it. Now, let's go play ball, man, you're holding us up!"

I was embarrassed and insulted by my brother's forwardness to solve my problem without my consent. So, after he walked out the room, I changed this, moved that over, and erased the way I started off, finished my remaining homework and went outside to play basketball. This made me very uncomfortable, because I viewed myself as a slow learner. He, on the other hand, was very competitive and unpredictable which I knew he would bring up later which would cause me to feel even more intellectually inferior. But I did it anyway.

The next day in school I turned in my assignment, the teacher graded it, the answer was correct. I was nervously excited because I could sense something else brewing. Well, just as I feared, Mrs. Pilot called out my name, "Finace!" I immediately went into a daze. "Finace

Bush," I sat numb as she asked, "Would you please go to the board and show us how you got your answer?"

I paused, getting up slowly while grasping my paper. "Without your paper" she said. There I was, partially leaning on my desk, looking despondent, and feeling exasperated in front of the entire class. I think I would have fainted had she not said, "That's ok Finace, we won't have time enough to finish before the bell rings." Oh my! What a temporary relief. Little did I know that things were about to change for me. God was doing something I could not have discerned in the slightest.

As I prepared to exit the class, my teacher, Mrs. Pilot, asked me to stay behind for a few minutes. Staring me in the center of my eyes, she asked, "Finace, did you do this or did someone else do it for you?" I replied, "Yes I did it but my sister helped me." Everyone at school knew my sister because she was a high achiever and very athletic. Piercing my heart with a blinkless stare, Mrs. Pilot said, "You don't have to be ashamed son, I've noticed how hard you work and I want you to keep working hard, it'll come."

Mrs. Pilot could see through my nervousness that something was wrong, but instead of embarrassing me she asked if I would like to meet with her during breaks or remain after class a few minutes a day to review assignments until I understood the basics. In retrospect, it became increasingly clear to me that receiving help from Mrs. Pilot was so significant and created a turning point in my life academically and spiritually. What began as a problem, turned out to be a great privilege. My light affliction, which was but for a moment, was working for me and if these sequence of events had not occurred I may not have gotten beyond my hidden fear that was rooted in deceitful pride.

It's interesting that the teacher named *Mrs. Pilot* was the one who demonstrated the kind of interest that encouraged me to "stay with it until I got the basics." And my younger brother, smarter than me academically, who advised me to "change that, move this, and erase that" were both used as catalyst to push me in the direction of my destiny.

I have used these two instructive disciplines many times in my life over the years, which came from two divinely appointed destiny travelers.

Reminiscent of my experience, I compared it with biblical truths that were revealed through prayer and meditation. In this, I discovered that God plants new beginnings through strange encounters.

GOD BIRTHS NEW BEGINNINGS
FROM STRANGE ENCOUNTERS

"Life is a maze for those who have no personal identity." In the sixteenth chapter and nineteenth verse of the Gospel of Matthew, Jesus said, *"I will give you the keys of the kingdom of heaven;"* (AMP). This phrase signified a kind of special power and divine right to Peter. Key's are important and significant symbols in life. Often, the person who has no key is not able to enter doors of opportunities.

In this case, the privilege of the keys meant that Peter would be a steward of the household of God; opening the door for men to enter into the Kingdom. Peter's response redefined his entire existence, unveiled his destiny, and set the stage for a life of purpose and fulfillment.

SELF-DISCOVERY IS THE KEY
TO PERSONAL FULFILLMENT

The critical key necessary for the consistent enjoyment of a fulfilled life is *self-discovery*. Many people have no idea who they are or what their purpose is, nor do they fully comprehend how to obtain these insights. I think the words of an anonymous patriarch says it best; "Usually a man does what he can until his destiny is revealed."

Jesus said to Peter: *"Peter, your name means a rock, and **your destiny** is to be a rock. You are the first man among the brethren to recognize me for what I am, and therefore you are the first stone in the edifice of the fellowship of those who are mine. In the days to come, **you must be the steward who unlocks the doors** of the kingdom that all men may enter."* (Matthew 16:18, 19)

HOW WE FUNCTION BEST

Peter made a discovery; however, along with his discovery he was given a great privilege and responsibility. It is a discovery that everyone must make for themselves and when this discovery is made, similar privileges and responsibilities are placed upon him. It is my conviction that we are all more effective when we function according to the uniqueness of our design instead of under the pressures we place on ourselves when attempting that which we are incapable of and lack the qualifications to perform.

Much like automobiles or high-tech devices, the potential of all humans can be greatly exploited or on the other hand appreciated if used according to the Creator's design and purpose.

Individuals who have not discovered their identity or purpose, in most cases, cannot discern where they fit, where they want to go in life, how to discern appropriate friendships and associations, the type of career paths that best satisfies their existence, or other critical issues that determine the quality of life.

Without knowing who we are, why we were created, or where we fit, it is very difficult to fulfill our God given purpose. Without purpose, we feel insignificant and unnecessary and ultimately make us vulnerable, frustrated, socially and morally bankrupt, easily offended, and self-destructive. So, I ask you, are you functioning according to the uniqueness of your design?

OUR BEST EXAMPLE

A close observation of Jesus' life illustrates the power and privilege of self-discovery:

"Now it happened as they journeyed on the road, that someone said to Him, "Lord, I will follow you wherever you go." And Jesus said to him, "Foxes have holes and birds of the air have nests, but the Son of Man has nowhere to lay His head." Then He said to another, "Follow

Me." But he said, "Lord, let me first go and bury my father." Jesus said to him, "Let the dead bury their own dead, but **you go and preach** *the kingdom of God." And another also said, "Lord, I will follow You, but let me first go and bid them farewell who are at my house." But Jesus said to him, "No one, having put his hand to the plow, and looking back, is fit for the kingdom of God" (Luke 9:57-62, NKJV).*

These things Jesus said to establish: *the urgency of kingdom business* and to ensure that *we maximize our potential by prioritizing our initiatives to correspond with our personal mission.* These passages also reflect the importance of time management which essentially is personal management. How you use your time today is a barometer for tomorrow's prosperity.

Jesus did not allow relationship crisis or conditions of urgency to alter his course. It was certainly God's will that determined His **direction,** His **timing**, and definitely His **priorities**. Notice that He kept his priorities on point in the story of Lazarus:

"Now **a certain man** *was sick, Lazarus of Bethany, the town of Mary and her sister Martha.* **It was that Mary who anointed** *the Lord with fragrant oil* **and wiped His feet** *with her hair, whose brother Lazarus was sick. Therefore* **the sisters sent to Him,** *saying, "Lord, behold, he whom you love is sick." When Jesus heard that, He said, "This sickness is not unto death, but for the glory of God, that the Son of God might be glorified through it." Now* **Jesus loved** *Martha and her sister and Lazarus. So,* **when He heard** *that he was sick,* **He stayed two more days in the place where He was.**

[Today, these circumstances, in many cases, would have required an urgent response and Jesus' seemingly insensitive lack of response would have been harshly judged.]

Then after this He said to the disciples, "Let us go to Judea again." The disciples said to Him, "Rabbi, lately the Jews sought to stone You, and are You going there again?" Jesus answered, "Are there not twelve hours in the day? If anyone walks in the day, he does not stumble, because he sees the light of this world. But if one walks in the night, he stumbles because the light is not in him." These things He said, and after that He said to them, "Our friend Lazarus sleeps, but I go that I may wake him up." Then His disciples said, "Lord, if he sleeps he will get well." However, Jesus spoke of his death, but they thought that He was speaking about taking rest in sleep. Then Jesus said to them plainly, "Lazarus is dead. And I am glad for your sakes that I was not there, that you may believe. Nevertheless let us go to him.

Then Thomas, who is called the Twin, said to his fellow disciples, "Let us also go, that we may die with Him." So **when Jesus came, He found that he had already been in the tomb four days.** *Now Bethany was near Jerusalem, about two miles away. And many of the Jews had joined the women around Martha and Mary, to comfort them concerning their brother.*

Now Martha, as soon as she heard that Jesus was coming, went and met Him, but Mary was sitting in the house. Now **Martha** *said to Jesus, "Lord,* **if You had been here,** *my brother would not have died. But even now I know that whatever You ask of God, God will give You." Jesus said to her, "Your brother will rise again. ..."*

... Then, when Mary came where Jesus was, and saw Him, she

*fell down at His feet, saying to Him, "Lord, **if you had been here,** my brother would not have died"* (John 11:1-32, NKJV).

Clearly, Jesus fully understood His mission. Understanding His mission allowed Him to direct His focus on daily priorities with laser-beam intensity. He was committed to accomplishing daily task without personal distractions or the demands of others near and dear to Him. His preparation and planning enabled Him to establish, what I refer to as, structured priorities which conditioned Him to *avoid confusion of responsibility and ownership of Himself.* He knew who He was and why He was sent, therefore, *He stayed on His course.*

You too must begin to experience a daily lifestyle that maximizes your personal uniqueness and ability. You must do so without infringing on the personal responsibility and assignments of others. Remember, confusion of our responsibility and ownership is due to a lack of *structured priorities.* This is a result of not knowing who you are.

FAILED ATTEMPTS:
STRIVING WITHOUT PRIORITIES

As overseer and mentor it is my most frequent observation that too often Believers take for granted the importance of managing their priorities and creating solid business habits which would allow them to prove to themselves that God really does bless them when they obey His Word.

For many years, I experienced blessings but had no tracking

systems to neither confirm nor measure God's involvement. I was like so many religious people who wonder why God does not seem to be concerned about their struggles, so they take life issues in their own hands and live as if their assessments are accurate. Proverbs 16:25 implies that what seems right are actually ways of death. In other words, each attempt makes their situation worst because good assumptions are not confirmed like truth.

Throughout this book I talk candidly about the life I experienced without managing my priorities effectively and the upgraded quality of life I now experience daily as a result of putting first things first. The Holy Spirit once said to me that "As long as you assume what's right, you will continue to live in error and forfeit God's best."

Here's the point you cannot miss; I am not implying that I was not reading , praying, studying, meditating, confessing, giving, doing good and living right as we sometimes say." The problem I had, like many others, is that although I was consistently carrying out my daily rituals and routines I was not working the Word of God effectively in my life that would have allowed it to shape my views and change my approach in the way I managed my affairs.

Some how I assumed that my ways were sufficient to guide and defend my life without even considering that God was only a ritual and religious practice I had included much like entertainment and sports. Once I got tired of reading and hearing what the Word said about my situations and looking at the differences in what it implied against my frustrated and bankrupt natural and spiritual life, I finally got it.

I knew I had a relationship with God because I was knowingly converted at age twelve, but things just weren't adding up. How could God possibly prove Himself to me when I was squandering everything He'd blessed me with?

After thirty years of attempting to be superman, spiderman, ghost-buster, lifesaver, the equalizer, and many other super-friends, I learned that life offers each of us opportunities. From these opportunities we either succeed or fail at them. How we decide to pursue them, and the standards and methods we apply to set our priorities determine the overall effectiveness of our impact on society. It also determines the daily level of joy and comfort we experience.

Therefore, our *structured priorities* should emanate based on our destiny and not as a temporary patch for the moment. Anyone who bases his or her response to life on crisis or favor that arises from a 'moment' may never know lasting success or the peaceful habitation that the Creator intended us to experience.

UNIQUENESS REQUIRES ATTENTION

We are all unique individuals. Some are exceptionally talented athletically and born with natural adroitness and agility that exceeds training. Some have perceptional gifts and skilled in multiple ways. Yet, there are some who possess skills and abilities but are searching to find their niche that makes them unique. They might search for the thing that not only makes them different, but will galvanize their passion with purpose and set them on a path to a peaceful and successful life.

Our development of that uniqueness ensures that we have the ability to contribute our uniqueness to the society designed by our awesome Creator. When we observe how a world map is structured to define boundaries for continents, countries, states, and cities, we see communities with physical property lines that distinguish ownership and preserve personal interest.

As a structured society, we must set spiritual, mental, emotional, and physical boundaries to define what is and is not our personal responsibility. Although you and I possess the skills necessary to perform certain tasks, without structured boundaries we lack the ability to adequately manage our time, money, relationships, and occupations.

The inability to structure our lives to maximize our potential and satisfy the demands of our existence is a serious problem. Failure to set appropriate boundaries at appropriate times with appropriate people is self–destructive behavior. Dedicated Believers are often confused about when it is 'biblically appropriate' to set limits or draw boundary lines when extending their 'undeveloped selves.'

AN EXPERIMENT THAT PAID DIVIDENDS

During the first three months of carefully observing my activities, I began structuring my daily functions. These are a few of the questions I was confronted with in the process:

1. Where do I begin?

2. What things should I consider first?

3. Is it possible to set limits and still be viewed as a loving person?

4. What if my family and close friends don't understand?

5. How will I respond to those who want my time, energy, or money when it is neither convenient nor appropriate for me?

6. Why do I feel guilty or afraid when considering potential conflicts with those who frequently interact with me?

7. How should structure apply to the roles within my marriage and parenting, daily devotion, exercise, work, ministry, diet, and rest so that I am effective?

8. Should I feel my need for "structure" is a selfish endeavor?

I was able to rediscover my true life and purpose through clear biblical references that addressed these questions specifically and silenced this internal ambivalence I contended with daily. It also delivered me from the turmoil and mediocrity that had dominated my life for so long. Sometimes ambivalent feelings that linger result from a lack of knowledge or uncertainty about individual rights and positions to take during certain exchanges with others close to you.

For example, during my young adult years I earned so much money through multiple streams of income that sometimes I would neglect my priorities to help my friends and associates who always seemed to struggle. At one time, I became a surety for three special friends, two preachers, and one relative. I had yet to learn that surety or co-signing for individuals was not wise according to the Scripture, especially for friends who did not have a proven record of faithfulness nor assets with enough value for collateral.

Proverbs 6:1 and 17:18 revealed to me that I was violating myself and my primary responsibilities for lacking wisdom of the Scriptures, assuming that God would have done the same thing. Like Jesus said in Matthew 22;29, *"You're off base on two counts:* You don't know your Bibles, and you don't know how God works."(The Message)

Only after the two preachers relocated miles away, ruined my credit, and left me with the responsibility of paying their debt, the Holy Spirit revealed what I was ready to learn. My teacher would often say to me, "Finace, when the student in you shows up, the teacher will emerge." At that time, life can use anything necessary to teach you.

This is a great reason to learn the principle of association to avoid unnecessary demands that others may impose on you through their access. I will discuss this principle in greater detail in the ingredients of "time, money and relationships."

This simplified revelation will empower you to regain ownership and responsibility of your "true self" through Kingdom principles empowered by the Holy Spirit. Self-discovery through Christ is an experience everyone should desire. It will rescue you from clinical psychological symptoms such as depression, anxiety disorders, eating disorders, addictions, impulsive disorders, guilt, problems in marriage and relationships with family and friends, which are deeply rooted in "you" due to a lack of understanding and need for a *structured lifestyle that corresponds with your expectations*. This revelation will enable you to understand proper ways to employ and apply faith to secure the manifestation of God's promises in your life.

My goal is to enable every Believer to realize that God has equipped each of us uniquely for success through the examples and patterns demonstrated by Christ and many others mentioned in His word. Before you complete this book it is my hope that you will agree with me that the only problem with structure is that you have lived too long without it!

The principle disciplines of structure are like ingredients designed to enhance you wholesomely through the ability to master your-self. Any attempt to master others is simply a waste of time.

Dr. Stephen R. Covey so eloquently stated, "Often in our relationships we want to control other people. At the same time, we resist their attempts to control us, scarcely remembering that if we resist control, they no doubt resist it as well. The fact is, neither we, nor they can be controlled by anyone else. We are each responsible for our own control."

Genesis 1:26 says, "And God said, *"Let us make man in our image, after our likeness: and let them have dominion over the fish of the sea, and over the fowl of the air, and over the cattle, and over all the earth, and over every creeping thing that creepeth upon the earth."*

Notice, God never said dominate, master, or lord over man. However, He did take precious time to identify the specific things of which mankind (*"them"*) is to share dominion. God must have been very serious about the specificity of this assignment because immediately after He created man, in verse twenty-seven, He reiterated His divine will for [them] man, in verse twenty-eight:

Notice, *"And God blessed them, and said to them, Be fruitful, and multiply, and replenish the earth, and subdue it: and have dominion over the fish of the sea, and over the fowl of the air, and over every living thing that moveth upon the earth."*

SOCIAL MALPRACTICE SELF ENRICHMENT LESSON

1. Let's reminisce. Think about an event that happened in your youth that served as a catalyst to help push you in the direction of your destiny. Is it still affecting your life? In what ways has it affected your life?

    _____

    _____

    _____

    _____

2. My self-discovery is the key to?

    _____

    _____

    _____

    _____

3. Have you discovered your Kingdom purpose? If yes, what were the attributing keys?

    _____

    _____

    _____

    _____

4. Why is it important to God that a person discover who they are, where they fit, where they want to go in life, how to discern appropriate friendships and associations, and the type of career path or occupation that would best satisfy their existence?

    _____

    _____

    _____

    _____

5. Based on Luke 9:57-62 (NKJV), how important are Kingdom priorities in the life of a Believer?

    _____

    _____

    _____

    _____

6. Based on Luke 9:57-62 (NKJV), how important is it to Jesus that we manage and prioritize our time?

    _____

    _____

    _____

    _____

7. Based on the section *"Best Example"* when a person desires to live according to the will of God, he/she must allow God to determine his/her _____, _____

    _____ and _____.

8. List a few spiritual keys that are/were instrumental in your spiritual development?

_____

_____

_____

_____

9. Are you viewed as a person who understands your mission and purpose? Why or why not?

_____

_____

_____

_____

10. Fill in the blank: Our structured priorities should be a:

_____ of _____

_____ and not a _____ -patch for

the _____.

11. How does having structured priorities relate to Genesis 1:28?

_____

_____

_____

_____

CHAPTER

4

THE POWER OF THE PATTERN

Now, if you followed closely through each of the points presented you probably realize that a **pattern** has been established for Kingdom citizens who are *"willing and obedient"* that guarantees **success**. Once you accept Jesus Christ as your Savior you are well on your way.

Scriptures clarify that God intended for each new Kingdom citizen to develop spiritually through discipleship designed to overcome issue after issue until our "being" and "doing" experience change. This is designed for each new convert to adopt the Kingdom's way as a new lifestyle.

The Bible carefully illustrates how Jesus (the ultimate example) who was faithful in prayer, Bible study, and discipline training, entered into His ministry filled with the Spirit, well prepared and qualified at the age of thirty.

Enlightened to His purpose, Jesus began fulfilling His mission. He also had a firm understanding of His Father's *will* through Scripture.

He called twelve others whom He mentored (trained and discipled) according to Kingdom principles. He supervised and navigated their development, while He accomplished His mission.

All established spiritual guides and instructors (pastors/teachers/ mentors) should assist in the development of students through teaching and training them to follow the example of Christ. The point here is that success should be second nature for Christians. Jesus left us a pattern that should be to convey through well-planned training sessions.

*"For I have given you an example, **that ye should do** as I have done to you"* (John 13:15, KJV).

*"Let this **mind** be in you, which was also in Christ Jesus: Who, being in the form of God, thought it not robbery to be equal with God:"* (Philippians 2:5, KJV).

"For even hereunto were ye called: because Christ also suffered for us, leaving us an example, that ye should follow his steps:" (1 Peter 2:21, KJV).

The Bible clearly teaches that when you walk according to the pattern that Christ has designed and left. This pattern dictates success in those specific areas. Not temporary success, but continued success throughout your life as you stay within this pattern.

WHAT HAS HAPPENED TO CHRISTENDOM!

Today, too many clergy and religious superiors are sporting and pleasing themselves by satisfying their personal, racial, and social agendas. Some use carnal reasoning and religious services that cater to their selfish desires and non-scriptural practices. This leaves the door open for demonic forces to gain ground by using schemes and devices that accelerate widespread satanic philosophies which can cripple the impact of the Word of God. Jesus addressed the religious leaders of His day for establishing similar services.

"Then came to Jesus scribes and Pharisees, which were of Jerusalem, saying, Why do thy disciples transgress the tradition of the elders? for they wash not their hands when they eat bread. But he answered and said unto them, Why do ye also transgress the commandment of God by your tradition? For God commanded, saying, Honor thy father and mother: and, He that curseth father or mother, let him die the death. But ye say, Whosoever shall say to his father or his mother, It is a gift, by whatsoever thou mightest be profited by me; And honour not his father or his mother, he shall be free. Thus have ye made the commandment of God of none effect by your tradition."
(Mathew 15:1-6)

Today, throughout the world in places of worship, we are faced with perplexities and diversities of troubles on every side resulting from the neglect and ignorance of essential principles. It is time for Kingdom Believers to begin aligning their operations and daily functions with Kingdom righteousness that pertains to godliness and fully corresponds with His will for us.

In order for any of us to experience effective Christianity, it must be understood that we must be trained as disciples to demonstrate God's way. It is a model way of doing and being that sets parameters for Believers' attitudes and practices to direct their destiny. In other words, it is to teach, train, and develop the spiritual fruit of discipline within each Believer. It is why Paul says, *"Follow me as I follow Christ."* Many times it's easier to communicate God's intentions by examples and illustrations, rather than oral and written lessons.

Those who fail to operate according to God's way because of traditions not inspired by God simply *"transgress the commandments of God"* by the man-made tradition, thus "making the commandment of God of no effect." These persons, according to Paul, have a zeal *for God, but not according to knowledge.*

Notice, they have a "zeal" (an intense enthusiasm and a passion; they are fanatics), *but, not according to what is proper and acceptable to God.* Here again, their methods, traditions, systems, practices, or convictions were not justified or authorized, therefore, could not be confirmed according to correct and vital knowledge.

"... For they being ignorant of God's righteousness, and seeking to establish their own righteousness, have not submitted to the righteousness of God." (Romans 10:2-3, NKJV). This is the result of non-effective, shallow Christianity.

Paul cautions the Colossians; *Beware lest any man spoil you through philosophy and vain deceit, after the tradition of men, after the rudiments of the world, and not after Christ.* (Colossians 2.8)

The Amplified version clarifies; *See to it that no one carries you off as spoil or make you yourselves captive by his so-called philosophy and intellectualism and vain deceit (idle fancies and plain nonsense), following* **human tradition** *(men's ideas of* **the material rather than the spiritual world),** *just crude notions following the rudimentary and*

elemental teachings of the universe and disregarding [the teachings of]
Christ (the Messiah).

As Believers we must make sure that what we extract from God's
Word reflects Christ and the standards, goals, and objectives He
communicated in His teachings, lest we lose the essence of the
Kingdom's way. *"Search the scriptures; for in them ye think ye have*
eternal life: and they are they which testify of me" (John 5.39).

SUCCESS SIMPLIFIED:
THE POWER OF THE PATTERN

In the Gospel of John chapter 13 verses 15-17, Jesus states that:
"For I have given you this as an example, so that you should do [in your
turn] what I have done to you. I assure you, most solemnly I tell you, a
servant is not *greater than his master, and no one who is sent is superior*
to the one who sent him. If you know these things, blessed and happy
and to be envied are you if you practice them [if you act accordingly and
really do them]" (AMP).

A closer examination of these passages allows us to see the
simplicity of Godly success. Notice in verse 15, Jesus first emphasizes
the importance of His example. The Webster Dictionary defines
"example" as something selected to show the nature or character of the
rest; a person or thing to be imitated modeled or patterned (Dictionary.
com, LLC s.d.).

Clearly, we may understand from this definition that Jesus

selected opportunities and events to show His disciples (followers) the importance of duplicating and imitating His pattern (example). In fact, verse 14 states that He obligated His disciples to imitate Him.

I must admit, this is where my life began to turn around in a way that allowed God to extend His grace into my life in a loving way. The Scriptures declare examples to be God's way of transferring Kingdom inheritance to the body of Christ.

Notice what Apostle Paul wrote to the Hebrew converts; *"In order that you may not grow disinterested and become [spiritual] sluggards, but imitators, behaving as do those who through faith (by their leaning of the entire personality on God in Christ in absolute trust and confidence in His power, wisdom, and goodness) and by practice of patient endurance and waiting are [now] inheriting the promises"* (Hebrews 6:12, AMP).

PREDESTINED AND GUARANTEED SUCCESS

Following a pattern practically guarantees, at a minimum, consistent results in most cases. So, if the pattern is positive the results are going to be positive, but if the pattern is negative the results are going to be negative. The success of every Believer has already been determined when we structure or lives to follow the biblical examples and patterns that Christ has patterned for us and sealed with His blood.

When a seamstress is contracted to make fifty choir robes, the initial design and structure of the first pattern may be difficult. But, after the first robe is completed, the other forty-nine becomes relatively easy and less time consuming due to the success of the first. This is also true in the case of blueprints and road maps. A blueprint may be difficult to draft, but upon completion, a builder only needs to be committed to following the details in order to construct a successful structure.

Most of us take great ease in getting into our automobiles and successfully traveling to and from our destinations. But how often are we mindful of the time, energy, and the number of lives that were sacrificed for our ease? Following an already established map (or pattern) is actually an accelerated guarantee to a successful journey.

This was the key to the success of the old patriarchs who succeeded Abraham; from Isaac to Joseph. The same concept or principle guaranteed Joshua's success. Joshua walked according to the predetermined laws that God had already established by his mentor, Moses.

THE KEY TO JOSHUA'S MINISTRY:
AN OLD TESTAMENT EXAMPLE

The success of Joshua's ministry was inevitable because of the blueprint established by Moses. God instructed Moses to take Joshua and transfer his spirit upon him. The Bible says that Joshua received the same spirit that was upon Moses (Numbers 27:15-23). Afterwards, when God visited Joshua, he immediately reminded him to do what Moses his mentor said, in order to succeed. This is found in Joshua 1:1-8:

"Now after the death of Moses the servant of the LORD it came to pass, that the LORD spake unto Joshua the son of Nun, Moses' minister, saying, Moses my servant is dead; now therefore arise, go over the Jordan, thou, and all this people, unto the land which I do give to them, even to the children of Israel.

Every place that the sole of your foot shall tread upon, that have I given unto you, as I said unto Moses. From the wilderness and this Lebanon even unto the great river, the river Euphrates, all the land of the Hittites, and unto the great sea toward the going down of the sun, shall be your coast.

There shall not any man be able to stand before thee all the days of thy life: as I was with Moses, so I will be with thee: I will not fail thee, nor forsake thee. Be strong and of a good courage: for unto this people shalt thou divide for an inheritance the land, which I sware unto their fathers to give them.

Only be thou strong and very courageous, that thou mayest observe to do according to all the law, which Moses my servant commanded thee: turn not from it to the right hand or to the left, that thou mayest prosper withersoever thou goest.

*This book of the **law shall not depart** out of thy mouth; but **thou shalt meditate** therein day and night, that thou mayest **observe to do** according to all that is written therein: for then thou shalt **make thy way prosperous,** and then thou **shalt have good success.***

Realize that true success has a blue print to follow. The route to it has already been established. There are many non-believers, discovering the way to secular success every day. Often, they use biblical information without a relationship with God and without a license to practice what's in the Book, while many Believers remain slothful and full of excuses. For that reason we need to look at 1 Corinthians chapter nine as one of the foundational scriptures to use in applying "structure." It is here that the Apostle Paul addresses the discipline it takes when striving for the mastery.

STRIVING FOR A MASTERY

In 1 Corinthians 9:25, Paul states: *"And every man that strives for mastery is **temperate** in all things...."* Paul asserts that we must commit ourselves to run in the race. But, we must "stop beating at the air." Each of us are uniquely fashioned with a distinct purpose and a chief aim in life. Discovering our purpose should motivate us to set clear goals. Those goals should be clarified and refined through the Word of God. Here Paul cautions Believers not to *beat at the* air, or in other words, waste time with things outside our central purpose; *"I don't fight an uncertain fight anymore,"* he says. To paraphrase what Paul is saying; I am not the feetattempting to perform as a hand. I am not a heart, acting like a liver. I study my purpose carefully based on how God designed me and the positions I hold. Then, by focusing my attention on who I am, I can then understand what I have to contribute.

Finally, with these things in perspective *I keep my body under* subjection to predetermined, corresponding disciplines lest I fail to accomplish that which is set before me. Life is filled with many issues.

Even so, the heart too has many issues to address. As the hard drive of a computer waits for instructions to be dictated to determine the function it will perform. So is the heart of man waiting for the correct instructions to be dictated from the Word of God to direct the proper ways to effectively function.

When wisdom suggests that we "guard our hearts with all diligence," the hint is to provoke us to be structured in every area pertaining to our personhood. Note that to further affirm this point, Wisdom strengthens her assertion by finishing this thought with *"for out of it are the issues of life!"*

This must be done in every personal and relational aspect of our manifest of life. We must begin with the prioritizing of our *three-part* or *triune* being. Then, properly assigning our time, we are to establish a mission for our money (resources) and clarify a vision for our family, develop the right attitude for work or occupation, and define our relationships to avoid unnecessary distractions and hindrances (using each of the principle ingredients of structure). This is what the Apostle Paul made clear in his first letter to the Believers at Corinth.

> *"Every Man that Striveth for the Mastery must be Temperate in all Things."*

Other scriptures that encourages Believers to follow the pattern:

- **1 Peter 2.21: Peter reiterated the importance and power of the pattern.**

For to this you were called [it is inseparable from your vocation]. *Because Christ also suffered for you, leaving you [it is personal]* **an example***, that* **you should follow** *on in His footsteps.* (NKJV)

For to this you were called, because Christ also suffered for us, leaving us **an example,** that we should **follow His steps** (NKJV). **The** Apostle Paul advises the church in several of his Epistles to follow the pattern that was established through Christ:

- **Hebrews 12:1-3 outlines a five-step concept** (discussed in greater detail in the chapter, "Lay Aside the Weight.")

  Therefore we also, since we are surrounded by so great a cloud of witnesses, let us lay aside every weight, and the sin which so easily ensnares us, and let us run with endurance the race that is set before us. **Looking unto** *Jesus, the author and finisher of our faith, who for the joy that was set before Him endured the cross, despising the shame, and has sat down at the right hand of the throne of God. For* **consider Him** *who endured such hostility from sinners against Himself, lest you become weary and discouraged in your souls.* (NKJV)

- **Philippians 2:5-8 outlines examples of Christ's humility in seven steps.**

  Let this mind be in you which was also in Christ Jesus, who, being in the form of God, did not consider it robbery to be equal with God, but made Himself of no reputation, taking the form of a bondservant, and coming in the likeness of men. And being found in appearance as a man, He humbled Himself and became obedient to the point of death, even the death of the cross.

- **Philippians 3:12-14 provides a three step description necessary to obtain the goal that lies ahead.**

   Not that I have already attained, or am already perfected: but I press on, that I may lay hold of that for which Christ Jesus has also laid hold of me. Brethren, I do not count myself to have apprehended; but one thing I do, forgetting those things which are behind and reaching forward to those things which are ahead, I press toward the goal for the prize of the upward call of God in Christ Jesus.

- *Philippians 4.8-9, defining the things necessary to set one's mind to be productive.*

   Finally, brethren, whatever things are true, whatever things are noble, whatever things are just, whatever things are pure, whatever *things are lovely, whatever things are of good report, if there is any virtue and if there is anything praiseworthy - meditate on these things. **The things which you learned and received and heard and saw in me, these do,** and the God of peace will be with you.*

- **Ephesians 6.11-17: The armor needed to conquer satanic and contrary forces.**

   Put on the whole armor of God, that you may be able to stand against the wiles of the devil. For we do not wrestle against flesh and blood, but against principalities, against powers, against the rulers of the darkness of this age, against spiritual hosts of wickedness in the heavenly places. Therefore take up the whole armor of God, that you may be able to withstand in the evil day, and having done all, to stand. Stand therefore, having girded you waist with truth, having put on the breastplate of righteousness, and having shod your feet with the preparation of the gospel of peace; above all, taking the shield of faith with which you will be able to quench all the fiery darts of the wicked one. And take the helmet of salvation, and the sword of the Spirit, which is the word of God;

- **Galatians 6.1-2: Paul outlines the application needed to restore fallen brethren.**

  Brethren, if a man is overtaken in any trespass, you who are spiritual restore such a one in a spirit of gentleness, considering yourself lest you also be tempted. Bear one another's burdens, and so fulfill the law of Christ.

There are many other patterns listed throughout the Scripture, which if applied, will generate significant Godly success!

CHAPTER

5

THE CURSE OF MEDIOCRITY

"A subtle time-induced stronghold is developed through
a disoriented state of mind; distorted by satanic deception
to rob God's people of their inheritance."
Finace Bush Jr.

If we are to live structured lives that will bring forth a fruitful Kingdom lifestyle, we must recognize what mediocrity is. Mediocrity is the acceptance of ineffectiveness of a method or systematic operation. In many cases, the processes consist of an unwillingness to abandon old practices or methods that no longer work.

It is much like the contemporary definition of **"insanity"** (doing the same thing, the same way, but expecting different results). It can become a hurdle in the life of every Believer who has not adopted God's Kingdom lifestyle. I call it the lifestyle of faith. If we accept anything as a way of life, as a system of belief and as a means of communicating or operating in this earth system *(other than what God says is an acceptable standard for life);* that is to operate in mediocrity. "Whatsoever is not of faith is sin." (Romans 14:23)

To expound further, **mediocrity** is neither implies good or bad according to Webster's Dictionary. In other words, to operate in mediocrity means to operate in the middle. The one place that God despises in the Kingdom is life in the middle.

In fact, in Revelation 3:15, 16, God says, *"I know your [record of] works and what you are doing; you are neither cold nor hot. Would that you were cold or hot! So, because you are lukewarm and neither cold nor hot, I will spew you out of My mouth!"* (AMP)

Sometimes this Scripture is taken out of context. God never said that you can't be cold, nor did He promote hot above cold. He said I'd rather you be either hot or cold. Listen, every church will not be hot, nor will every church be cold. If you study the passage in context you will see that the region the text is extracted from had two climates in it. One climate was very cold; the other climate was very hot.

Jesus said neither one of those climates bothered God, He likes both. There is a time when heat is the very thing I need, there is also a time when cold is the appropriate climate. But what He doesn't like is the in-between. It makes God sick. In my personal opinion, lukewarm climates or in-between weather conditions generate more sicknesses and viruses than any other seasonal conditions each year.

MEDIOCRE PEOPLE ARE NOT SUCCESSFUL

Mediocrity is also defined as ordinary; to be average. It's amazing how many Believers are satisfied with being average. They commonly feel as though they are like everybody else. This is a disoriented mindset. This type of closed-mind keeps a person estranged and alienated from the life God has predestined for them.

The reality of salvation means that there is an anointing on life that makes everyone better than before. No longer are we common persons as spouses, parents, pastors, sons, brothers, friends, on the job, during leisure, recreational activities, nor in any other necessary functional lifestyle situation where performance is an issue.

You must realize that as a child of God,

you are a new class of people!

"Transformed from the kingdom of darkness

into the kingdom of light.

A royal priesthood, a peculiar nation,

and a chosen generation of people."

Mediocrity means ordinary; average;

"NOT GOOD ENOUGH" (Dictionary.com).

It means that you don't have the kind of structure that enables you to rise or succeed. The ability, through your own philosophy, to rise above ordinary or common crisis in life is not there. **You tell yourself you're not good enough.**

It also means the acceptance of inferiority; it's the absence of ability to compete with others because you don't realize you possess what it takes. You can't imagine yourself living in above average conditions. You don't have enough wind beneath your wings to fly. It says that you are just not cut out for it. Mediocrity is a curse!

In his Epistle to the Ephesians, Paul encourages Believers to make sure they have the right mindset to avoid alienation or being cut off from the life of God because of ignorance.

*This I say therefore, and testify in the Lord, that ye henceforth walk not at other Gentiles walk **in the vanity of their mind,** having their understanding darkened, being **alienated** from the life of God **through the ignorance** that is **in them, because of the blindness** of their **heart**: Who being past feeling have given themselves over unto lasciviousness, to work all uncleanness with greediness. But **have not so learned Christ;** If so be that ye have heard him, and have been taught by him, as the truth is in Jesus: That ye put off concerning the former conversation the old man, which is corrupt according to the deceitful lusts; And **be renewed in the spirit of your mind;** Ephesians. 4:17-23 (KJV)*

The most significant reason that mediocrity must not be practiced from the Believers is because it *is a subtle time induced stronghold developed in a disoriented state of mind, distorted by satanic deception, to rob God's people of their inheritance.*

Mediocrity is the dysfunctional system that keeps Kingdom citizens bound to poverty stricken, menial, and non-progressive conditions.

Their lack of knowledge usually results in disenfranchised citizenship. It is the only futile mind-set that suggests that we can never work in a better job, culture, or climate because of presumed limitations. That we cannot move up in life. That we should never dream of living in better houses or owning more than one at a time.

It also suggests that we cannot own luxurious and sporty cars while living in extravagant homes, while striving to please God. That we certainly cannot clothe ourselves in high-fashion apparel and own these things at the same time. Remember, the Bible emphatically states that *"the earth is the Lord's!"*

OTHER DIABOLICAL SATANIC EFFECTS OF MEDIOCRITY

Mediocrity also prevents talented people from even dreaming of starting their own companies or developing concepts and ideas that may be worth millions. It prevents God-inspired insights that could acquire freedom and create better opportunities for families, friends, and others throughout communities.

The good news is, you don't have to accept that the job you have is where you must stay for the next forty years because it's what your parents did. You do not have to accept living in the same starter home for the rest of your life just because your immediate family and neighborhood peers expect you to. Neither do you have to succumb to the limits that some misguided religious and secular persons will try to impose on you.

God's promises yield provision for those who work according to his plan. "He came that you might have life and that more abundantly." The truth is, God's desire is to see you live life as He lives it. Remember, you are His child and as with earthly Fathers, they desire for their children to live a qualitative and purposeful life.

GOD'S ULTIMATE DESIRE: TO GIVE YOU THE GOOD LIFE!

In John 10.10, Jesus made a very insightful declaration. *"I have come that you may have life and that you may have it more abundantly."* Note, the word He used for "life" in the original Greek is "Zoe¨," denoting life as a principle, life as God has it; that which the Father has in Himself and that which He gave to His son to have in Himself.

In other words, God's purpose for sending His Son was to give us "Life" as He lives it through a system called Kingdom righteousness. This is the primary reason Jesus encouraged all new converts to first seek the Kingdom of God and His righteousness. It is through the Kingdom of God's system that we rediscover the God life which is actually the proper way to live.

To further support this claim, notice John 5.26 of the Amplified: *"For even as the Father has life in Himself and is self-existent, so He has given to the Son to have life in Himself and be self-existent."*

"This I say therefore, and testify in the Lord, that ye henceforth

*walk not as other Gentiles walk, in the vanity of their mind, Having the understanding darkened, being **alienated from the life of God through the ignorance** that is in them, because of **the blindness of their heart:"*** (Ephesians 4.17, 18).

THE HOLY SPIRIT ALSO CRIES OUT THROUGH THE APOSTLE IN ROMANS 12:1, 2

*"I beseech you therefore, brethren, by the mercies of God that you present your bodies a living sacrifice, holy, acceptable unto God, which is your reasonable service. And be not conformed to this world: but be ye transformed **by the renewing of your mind**, that ye may prove what is that good and acceptable and perfect will of God."*

Ephesians 2.10 (AMP)
*"For we are God's [own] handiwork (His workmanship), recreated in Christ Jesus, [born anew], that we may **do those good works** which God predestined (planned beforehand) for us, [taking paths which He prepared ahead of time] **that we should walk in them [living the good life** which He prearranged and made ready for us to live]."*

A very substantial part of this life is realized and discovered through the preaching and teaching of the gospel. However, in many religious institutions, these Scriptures are never mentioned, causing many who lack the faith necessary to experience such a lifestyle to forfeit God's provision because they never heard it. Romans 10:17 states: "So then faith cometh by hearing, and hearing by the word of God."

A LESSON FROM THE COMICS

In the comic strip, Superman, there is a depiction of a seemingly common man that allows insight into the real (spirit) man; beneath the surface and is on standby daily waiting for a crisis to arise. These situations allow him to demonstrate his uncommonly supernatural abilities among common people.

Let's look at superman. He is an extraordinarily powerful man among a class of people distinguished as super friends. Each of the super friends operated like normal ordinary citizens. Until these cataclysmic events occurred and buildings began falling, trains derailing, cars and trucks crashing and the crowds began frantically losing control.

Many people were screaming and some were fleeing without instruction, others were panic-strickened, and terrified. In the midst of the horrific noises and chaos, suddenly, the real man burst out of the calamity and began controlling, rescuing, directing, and taking charge of an out of control situation. As a whisper of wind demanded the attention of the masses, someone shouted "look! It's a bird, it's a plane, it's Superman!"

It was all, the otherwise known, Clark Kent needed. Do you remember the bumbling idiot working at the Daily Planet, stumbling around clumsily pursuing Lois Lane? Lois knew she liked him, but he never manifested anything other than nerdish tendencies, so she was uninterested. In the midst of crisis Lois is uninhibited in her enticement to the person that looks just like Superman, but the difference is he has an "S" on his chest and now instead of the problem managing him; he is now exercising dominion over the problem.

NOW, THE LESSON

What was the comic saying? Was he saying that the difference between Superman and us is that when pressure comes he allows it to make him, while it breaks you? Let me tell you something, the cycle of life is on this wise; while you are having trouble with your problems, someone else is triumphing over you through them because they generate what you need in order to correct your problem. So you pay them to deal with your problems. You would drown in them if someone else didn't create a lifeline to deliver you.

The mediocre state of mind is the mind that says I can't survive without the assistance of others. Friends you must learn that there is a "greater" that lives inside of you that can turn your troubles into triumphs, your valleys into mountains, and your problems into pleasures.

Paul promises that God will not allow you to encounter more than you were built to handle. "...But will, with the temptation (test and trial) also make a way to escape, that you may be able to bear it." John says that "whatsoever is born of God overcomes the world and this is the victory that overcomes the world, even our Faith". Many times Believers fail to properly evaluate crisis that arise in life.

UNDERSTANDING CRISES

Many times Believers are crippled because they fail to understand that crises in life are not unique situations designed to erode their courage or confidence. However, they are opportunities that enable Believers to demonstrate Christ, to show non-believers why it is essential to have such a strong man and strong word within.

Even the wisest, strongest, most noble and most successful patriarchs, kings, queens, presidents, scholars, and professionals have suffered chapters of heartbreak and failure. Commonly they, like us, have learned that victory does not come without valleys, power is not generated without pressure, and true gain is the result of sometimes many losses and that failure is many times the womb of success which is the price we all pay for living.

Believers who allow disappointments and defeats to dissolve their faith (trust) in God will always remain in the shadows of others, hiding behind sorry apologies and excuses while the years waste away. An anonymous writer once stated that "Success, when it comes overnight, often departs with the dawn. Therefore, failure is, in a sense, the highway to success." The Apostle Paul conveyed insights about the Believer's ability to prevail through Christ.

Paul's Perspective

In his second letter to the Corinthians Paul stated that we have a treasure within us to show that this power, ability, and light we manifest through crises is from God and not from us.

But we have this treasure in earthen vessels, that the excellency
of the power may be of God, and not of us.
We are troubled on every side,
yet not distressed; we are perplexed, but not
in despair; persecuted but not forsaken;
cast down but not destroyed; always bearing about in
the body the dying of the Lord Jesus that the life also of Jesus
might be made manifest in our body.
2 Corinthians 4:7-10 (KJV)

Notice the Amplified;
"However, we possess this precious treasure,
the divine light of the Gospel, in frail, human vessels of earth
that the grandeur and exceeding greatness of the power may be shown
to be of God and not from ourselves. We are hedged in,
pressed on every side, troubled and oppressed in every way;
but not cramped nor crushed; we suffer embarrassments and are
perplexed and unable to find a way out, but not driven to despair;
We are persecuted and hard driven, pursued but not deserted to stand
alone; strucked down to the ground, but never struck out destroyed;

Always bearing about in the body, the liability and exposure to
the same putting to death that the Lord Jesus suffered. So that the
resurrection life of Jesus also, may be shown forth by,
and in our bodies."
(2 Corinthians 4:7-10, AMP)

The thing that Paul is saying in this passage is that there is another "you" inside of you, but you've gotten so accustomed to catering to the one you see that you never expect the inner person to take over. In this case, to be mediocre means to never expect anything better than what you are already accustomed to experiencing on a daily basis.

Some people have had (just) enough bad experiences to expect bad situations to continue to occur. They only use their imagination to expect more bad experiences. Then they constantly speak death in accordance with what they imagine; conditioning themselves to live hopelessly.

Other Believers will never try to do certain things again because they have been convinced through past experiences that new methods, new systems, and new ideas won't work. These improper assessments or false evaluations carry over into too many areas of their life setting the stage for a life dominated by mediocrity.

We must realize that crisis provides opportunities for Believers, who live by faith, to manifest the ability of Christ that is within.

Satan knows that he doesn't have to send demons to disrupt many converts. There are a few people in the church that get most of the demonic activity. There are many people in the church who will never need demonic coercion; they do the devil's job for him, without any coercion or suggestion. Simultaneously, they perform demonic activities. Mediocrity here means that they have accepted things the way they are and are not open to anything new, even though the systems they employ are not effective.

Many people get satisfaction out of just having somebody they can talk to about problems they face. They sit around chatting about the latest news, never discussing even a hint of what they can do to stop it.

When new ideas and concepts are generated that has the potential to change the situations they are tired of, they persecute them because their "limited vision" is subjected to a closed mind dominated by mediocrity.

Mediocrity cannot accept what it cannot see. This means that a blind state of mind has accepted a lie from the pit that things will not change despite attempts to make life better.

MIND BLINDNESS

According to Paul in Ephesians 4:17 "I'm urging you to stop walking like other Gentiles walk." How did they walk? In the vanity or futility of their minds; do you know what the vanity of the mind is?

It is the mind that has never been taught what the life of God is and therefore has no conviction to prepare itself to know. It is the mind that is bent on being common with life as it was prior to the experience of salvation. It is the mind that has never believed that it can quit falling victim to the same habits.

Remember, anyone who becomes a part of a new system, society, or culture without proper orientation, will be dysfunctional and eventually disenfranchised. Let's call it the "curse of the 3 Ds": disoriented, dysfunctional, and disenfranchised. This description fits a large percentage of the religious community. The primary reason that some habits keeps Kingdom citizens bound is because they were never properly yoked to Christ to learn His ways. As a result, they fail to realize the power within to change through Christ. This is the primary reason Hosea said that God's people are destroyed for a lack of knowledge.

LIFE WITHOUT PROPER ORIENTATION
The devastation of attempting godly pursuits the wrong way!

Have you ever been in a good fight before? Have you ever fought a fight and lost? Many times the pain of losing teaches us not to attempt things the same way again. Especially if you learned to fear defeat before you were taught the proper way to fight. Consider this; Mediocrity had settled in as a stronghold in the mind simply because of the absence of a proper orientation of life.

Satanic and worldly reasoning infiltrated many minds, establishing improper thought patterns that through time have shaped the way the majority of our religious society functions. What has become **normal** to many is now the thing they **value**. The thing they *value* has become their **standard**. Their *standards* have constructed their **beliefs** which have shaped their **convictions** and now their *convictions* are determining their constant **responses**.

Another factor that must be included is decisiveness. Now, if you have ever run up against a real good obstacle or hurdle before and it hurt you, you learned not to do that again. The energy and reasoning it took for you to make that decision is called **decisiveness**.

It's unimportant what pushed you to the point of becoming decisive; you became decisive about it and never repeated it. After we are properly orientated, we should be decisive in asserting the power and wisdom we've gained through orientation to take control and exercise dominion over habits that dominate us.

The only thing wrong with the ugly habits someone have may exist as a result of alcohol, smoking, crack, smack, methyl, seaweed, bennies, red devils, uppers, or downers. It doesn't matter what it is, when someone is decisive and stands upon God's Word, the "ugly habit" cannot subdue you any longer.

Now, as you walk by faith in the Word, refuse to open the door to your heart and emotions any longer to negatives. If you take the instructions from the Word of God for granted, that's mediocrity—and it means you don't mind having an excuse to hide behind to use as a reason not to change. This kind of complacent thinking cripples millions of strong, educated, and gifted individuals. In the case of Believers, this type of thinking is called walking in the vanity of the mind. It is a state of mind that opposes the truth of God about life.

WINNING OVER MEDIOCRITY
BY IMPLEMENTING STRUCTURE

Remember, it may be difficult in the beginning to conquer mediocrity. But it is important to remind yourself that you must persist until you succeed. You may have already tried other systems or methods to conquer bad habits but to no avail. When implementing structure, pay particular attention in the first few days and it is likely you will be able to identify the ills of your own life.

First, you will be able to determine *why* you have the kind of problems you do. Then, you will discover the importance of paying attention. However, be mindful that until you personally identify those things that challenge your progress, you will keep experiencing the same crisis. Commit to structuring your lifestyle in such a way that God is glorified through your obedience to His Word. Within four-to-six weeks, you will begin to experience personal growth and power. If you have a problem managing your time effectively, prioritizing your relationships, finances, and other critical areas, you will have a problem prioritizing your "triune" [three-part] man; spirit, soul, and body.

Remember, your tri-unity is prioritized by honoring your spirit-man first. If your decisions are not based on the regard of your spirit-man first, then you set yourself up for defeat. The way that you gage success through the spirit-man is to make sure that whatever the whole-man is getting ready to do, lines up with the Word of God.

The **spirit of man** is first, the **soul of man** is second, and the **body of man** is last.

Here is an example: If we implement a physical structure in our life first through exercise, our physical body will become stronger than our spirit. Because of this, a spiritual devotion first is imperative to prepare and equip us for our physical endeavors. We must **"commit our way to the Lord and our work shall be established."**

Some people want to have a sound operation but they go about it in an unsound and ineffective way. The Bible says, **"First seek the Kingdom of God** and its righteousness and all these other things shall be added."

MEDIOCRITY IS A STATE OF MIND

Why are some Believers stuck in sin, sickness, and poverty, even though the price of redemption has been paid and the Gospel emphatically proclaims our deliverance? Certainly the curse of the 3-Ds exposes many contributing factors.

The heart (spirit) must be established in faith, by the Word of God, and the mind must be prepared to attract the reality it desires from the Word. It is only after this that real change will manifest. True success in any area, especially for the inexperienced, will require continuity of thought and passionate desire that generates strong focus.

There is also a difference in wishing for a "thing" and being ready to receive that "thing." None of us are really ready for just *anything* until we believe we can acquire it. Belief is essential. A person also needs activities that connect them from day-to-day to their aspirations as well as their thoughts.

Where there are too many breaks, people tend to lose sight of their goals. This may lead to frustration and confusion. Some actually fail because too many breaks dissolved the passionand momentum they started with. Do you believe that you can acquire the promises in the Word? The Word of God proves that people whose lives hardly ever receive these promises actually disappoint and anger God (see Hebrews 3:4 and Numbers 13:14).

Noah Example

God said to Noah, "Build me an ark"... Noah asked "Why?" God replied "Because rain is coming." Noah said, "Lord I've never seen the rain." God told Noah not to worry and said, "I'll show it to you, and you just commit to building the ark ... and conform your activities to whatever it takes to manifest the ark as an earthly reality. At the appointed time you will see the rain when you are sheltered in the Ark."

The Ark of Provision

The same day that God gave Noah the promise of provision for his present crisis was the same day He gave Noah the promise of provision for his future; to secure his eternity.

Many have sadly misunderstood that the promise of faith is just as much a provision for now as it is against tomorrow's end of age. The problem some have is that they believe God has delivered them from the fires of hell through the blood of Jesus, and that they may go to Heaven. However, they do not realize that same promise that allowed Noah to escape the future damnation (the flood) was the same promise (the ark) that sustained Him during the stormy rain. In other words, the ark was filled with the abundance of God's provision.

There was not one animal on the boat that had to eat the other, neither did Noah's family eat meat. Noah believed God and moved! Noah structured his life around the promise. And as he structured his life he was able to complete the tasks God had given him.

It impacted his life, the lives of his family, and the generations that followed. So, structuring your life will potentially impact the lives of others associated with you for generations!

Let's Be Real!

Ironically, many Believers today would not believe if God said to them that they can have an uncommon blessing. Most would be so dominated by mediocre thinking and closed minds that they would likely discount it as God for the three basic reasons listed earlier. I called it "DDD"; the three crippling Ds of Christianity; disoriented, dysfunctional, and disenfranchised.

Understanding Faith

Your faith needs to have mission when God assigns a promise to you. The reason He gives a promise is because contained within the promises are provisions. One has to structure their lives around the promise in order to access the provision within it. This provision is two-fold when accessing through true faith: First, provision is for now (the present); second, it is for later (eternity). Jesus confirms this fact in Mark 10.30: *"he shall receive a hundredfold now in this time....and in the world to come eternal life."* God has provided everything we need, yet, as a church we haven't gotten serious about accessing it.

The religious community can be lazy, complacent, disoriented, and dysfunctional at times; a system that will remain disenfranchised if it ceases to seek God for direction. Recognize that God has done for all, but all are not trying to do for themselves. Therein lies a successful tactic among the enemy's arsenal.

The Process

We are not ready for a "thing" until we believe that we can acquire that "thing." It is the state of our mind and condition of our spirit that determines whether we live in mediocrity or by faith. A person's state of mind must be one of belief not merely wishful thinking. A closed mind cannot inspire faith. It doesn't matter what is preached or taught, if your mind is closed it can't receive. Therefore, it is essentially impossible to bring it to pass because you aren't able to see it inside of you.

There are actually people who are seriously addicted to self deception because of an unstructured lifestyle that promotes mediocrity. This may be due to their personal philosophy of life. However, they desperately need organized thoughts (structure) aligned with the Word of God to produce or manifest the things they believe for by faith.

When the right applications are made, there is no more effort needed to aim high in life to demand abundance and prosperity from life, than is required to settle for mediocrity. I've learned that "misery and poverty" cost the same amount of time and energy that success and abundance does. It is a matter of how you bargain with life and what principles you decide to engage.

The body of Christ must begin to experience and walk daily in what the Bible identifies as our inheritance. God intends for Kingdom citizens to become *"Cities on a hill that cannot be hid."* Which actually implies that we become high stations in the earth through our commitment to Kingdom principles and that, in turn, will a attract non-believers to God, through Christ.

We cannot walk out this principle with a mediocre mentality. Jesus said *"I came that you might have life and that more abundantly."*

CHAPTER
6

PRIORITIZING MY TRI-UNE OR THREE-PART MAN

"But seek ye first the Kingdom of God, and his righteousness;
and all these things shall be added unto you"

Imagine that you are about to begin construction on a housing project. Where would you start? Suppose you have gotten all the materials delivered to the site, everything's scattered in bundles and heaps, but this is your first time attempting a project of this magnitude. What would you do? First thing to know is; don't panic! So, starting a critical project such as prioritizing your tri-une (or three-part) man, where will you start? How does one start such an enormous project when everything seems to be in such disarray? Again, don't panic! I will share with you how to accomplish such an important task. There is a practical way to achieve a successful construction project. It is a tested and proven system (or method) drafted from the Master Creator's manual detailing how to do things successfully. You actually need the same process that the wisdom of God employed to renovate the earth.

This is discovered in Genesis chapter one.

Structure is the master key to success! The process of setting your house in order, getting things arranged like they ought to be. To structure something means to actually build or to construct something. It is made up of a number of parts arranged together. In this case I want you to think about how you were made, who made you and why. In other words, why are you here?

THE THREE DIMENSIONS OF MAN

There are three dimensions of humans that have to be properly structured before anyone can fully discover their God-given purpose. Those dimensions are spirit, soul and body. The spirit man, the soul man and the body (or natural man) must be structured and functioning in proper order to experience a wholesome life.

One primary reason I emphasize the term **structure** is because each day I associate with some of the most prominent and talented people in this society. Some have an abundance of potential, yet never really exploit their inherent abilities because they accept counter-intentional and dysfunctional lives. Many others never bother to take the time to look into the owner's manual (God's Holy Word) to determine how or why they were made.

From the Owner's Manual Perspective

The Bible teaches that God made all men for Himself, for His own glory. This means that you and I were not designed to decide what was best for us without our Creator's input. Each time we purchase an instrument or piece of equipment that has several different functions; we need the owner's manual to instruct us of its proper use. In this case, the owner's manual is not something written by the user, but *for* the user. It was dictated by the originator/designer of the instrument from whom we were purchased.

It is necessary to examine what the owner has to say about proper use of this instrument because when we fail to do so, we risk damaging our goods. This happens when we lack the ability to properly and affectively use what we purchased.

Another basic reason to apply structure is to identify the way God (our owner) prioritizes our three-part being and discover the part of our being He dwells in so that we can develop an intimate relationship with Him.

Man is not only what he sees, but there is more to man than what meets the natural eye. Man is a spirit that has a soul, which lives in a body. Since we are spirit-beings first, we must recognize the need to develop our spirit man first (John 6:63).

I'm sure you know several Believers who have spent countless time and energy trying to bring their bodies to submission to God's way. They fail to understand that the natural man or body is the only part of our triune man at death that will be shed as the spirit and soul returns back to God.

So many Believers focus the majority of their time, energy, and resources on natural pursuits and comforts. Rather than focusing their time, energy, and resources into spiritual development and submission to the Kingdom of God and His righteousness.

There are three steps that must be taken to properly establish the priorities of the triune man. First, the natural man (body) or *sarkinoi* must be forced into submission to the will of God to conform to whatever target or goal he tries to accomplish from the Word of God. It is safe to say; "No force, no conformance." Second, man's mind (soul) or *psuche*, which is comprised of five faculties; thoughts, feelings, intellect, will, and disposition must be renewed by using the methods from Joshua 1:8 and Psalm 1:1-3 to dictate acceptable thoughts and images that correspond with man's desired pursuits.

This is to first control the rational part of man's soul which consists of thoughts and intellect. As man does this, he must simultaneously set his affections or emotions which marinates and incubates thoughts to align or agree with God-inspired pursuits so it becomes abundant to him. This is the process of setting affections on the things above.

Thirdly, the heart (spirit) or *pneuma* must be established and allowed to function as the chief of the three-part man. Successfully completing these three critical steps will allow the triune function properly. So, what are you waiting for? You are only three steps away from structure!

THE NATURAL MAN MUST BE FORCED
INTO SUBMISSION

Romans 8.8 implies that to live according to the flesh is to live a life dominated by the dictates and desires of a sinful human nature. The flesh here is referred to as man's *lower nature* (his body or natural mind influenced by satanic and worldly advice). Notice that "the flesh **cannot** please God.

> *So then they that are in the **flesh** cannot please God.*
> *But you are not in the flesh, but in the*
> *Spirit, if so be that the Spirit of God dwell in you.*

This is a very emphatic statement that factors very heavily in a Believer's ability to experience prosperity in the Kingdom of God. Since this is the case at hand, Paul insists that a life dominated by such dictates and desires leaves a person vulnerable to the *works of the flesh*, mentioned in Galatians 5:19-21, further declaring that *"they which do such things shall not inherit the Kingdom of God."* Each of these passages outlines the necessity of body subjection. In Paul's first letter to Corinth, he explains the importance of bringing the body into compliance of God's Word to be worthy of receiving the prize.

*Know ye not that they which run in a race run all, but one receiveth the prize? So run, that ye may obtain. And every man that striveth for the mastery is **temperate** in all things. Now they do it to obtain a corruptible crown; but we an incorruptible. I therefore so*

run, not as uncertainly; so fight I, **not as one that beateth the air: But**
I keep under my body, and bring it into subjection: *lest that by any*
means, when I have preached to others, I myself should be a castaway.
(1 Corinthians 9:24-27 KJV)

Here Paul compares himself to the racers and combatants in the
games well known to the Corinthians. Those who ran in their games
were placed on a strict diet and had to exercise extreme discipline. In
Paul's mind they are the examples of how Believers should likewise
abstain from fleshly appetites and heathenistic sacrifices for the
heavenly crown.

Those who fought with one another in these exercises prepared
themselves by beating the air, as the Apostle calls it, or by throwing out
their arms and thereby injuring themselves beforehand to better prepare
themselves for close combat.

There is no room for any such exercise in Christian warfare.
Christians are always in close combat. Our fleshly enemies make fierce
and hearty opposition and are in constant pursuit of our bondage. For
this reason, Believers must remain earnest and never drop out of the
contest, nor attempt to retire from it. We must fight, not as those that beat
the air, but we must strive against the strongholds with all our might.

Paul mentions one contemptible enemy; the body (or the natural
man). The body must be kept under, beaten black and blue (as the
combatants were in the Grecian games) and constantly brought into
subjection. By the "body," Paul is speaking of fleshly appetites and
inclinations. Everyone who will pursue the interest of their souls must

be committed to beat their bodies into compliance. They must endure hard combat against fleshly lusts until they are subdued. **The body must be made to serve the mind** as it is renewed by spiritual principles and not be allowed for a moment to lord over it.

YOUR MIND MUST BE RENEWED AND YOUR AFFECTIONS SET ON HIGH THINGS

In other words, a person's thoughts need to be tried and their feelings need weighed because of the potential deception of both. Just because a person becomes a Believer does not mean that the way they think or feel instantly becomes godly or right.

Entry into any new arena or phase of life requires proper orientation. This is true in relationships, cultural changes, professions and career paths, new equipment and upgrades in technology. This has certainly been neglected in Christianity far too long. It appears to me that if industries and corporations understand the significance of employee orientation and training before allowing new employees to operate, the Body of Christ should at least realize that new converts must be orientated and trained as well.

Importance of Orientation

It is no wonder Jesus said of the Scribes and Pharisees that they go through discomforting difficulties to get one follower only to make the person two times worst. This is spiritual assassination and should not exist in the Body of Christ. They have failed to renew their minds.

Any organization, group, club, or Church that desires to progress, expand, or grow (including personnel recruitment) must understand the priority of orientation. In most performance-based organizations, when a new employee is disoriented, they are dysfunctional in that organization and will eventually become disenfranchised. These three Ds are responsible for most of the devastation occurring in the Christian community than any other satanic implant.

Mind Renewal Begins With Orientation

Without orientation a person really does not know what to expect. They are not aware of purposes, goals, missions, policies, practices, systematic functions, or performance expectations within the new affiliation. Orientation sets the stage for the essential parts of a lesson or a task to be conveyed and grasped with less difficulty.

In these two verses Paul gives practical advice to the Believers in Rome. They should offer their bodies and *mind to prove God's will*. Paul urges the Believers at Rome to engage true worship; not as a ritual or noble act.

As the well-known commentator, William Barkley, wrote; "Real worship is the offering of everyday life to him, not something transacted in a church, but something which sees the whole world as the temple of the living God."

A person may say, I am going to church to worship God, but he should also be able to say, I'm going to work, the store, the restaurant, to the park, the game, the neighbors house, the mall, and anywhere else he goes to worship God. After orientating the Romans with an earnest discussion about reasonable service to open their minds, Paul begins to demand radical change. Why? Because he knew that a Godly message could not be effectively communicated to a closed natural mind.

And be not conformed to this world: but be ye transformed by **the renewing of your mind,** *that ye may prove what is that good, and acceptable and perfect will of God.*

To express this idea he uses two, almost untranslatable, Greek words; ***suschemati-zesthai****,* which means to be conformed to this world. The root of this word is ***schema****;* meaning the outward form that varies from day-to-day and year-to-year.

Barkley writes "A man's ***schema*** is not the same when he is fifteen-years-old as it is when he is fifty. It is not the same when he goes out to work as it is when he is dressed for dinner; it is continuously altering. So Paul says, "Don't try to match your life to all the fashions of this world; don't be like a chameleon which takes its color from its surroundings."

The word he uses for being transformed from the world is ***metamorphousthai.*** Its root is ***morphe****,* which means the essential unchanging shape or element of a thing. A man has not the same schema at fifteen and fifty, but he has the same ***morphe***. A man in blue jeans has not the same ***schema*** as a man in evening attire but they have the same ***morphe***. His outward form changes, but inwardly he is the same person. So, Paul says, to worship and serve God, we must undergo a change, not of our outward form but of our inward personality. What is this change?

Paul would say that left to ourselves we live a life of **kata sarka**, dominated by human nature at its lowest. In Christ we live a life of **kata Christon** or **kat pneuma**, dominated by Christ or by the Spirit. The essential man has been changed. Now, he lives, not a self-centered but, a Christ-centered life. This must happen by the renewal of his mind.

The Word he uses for renewal is **anakainosis**. In Greek there are two words for "new"-- **neos** and **kainos**. Neos means new in point of time; **Kainos** means new in point of character and nature. A newly manufactured pencil is **neos**; but a man who was once a sinner and is now on his way to being a saint is **kainos**. When Christ comes into a man's life he is a new man; his mind is different, because the mind of Christ is in him.

When Christ becomes the center of a person's life then this person can present real worship, which is the offering of every moment and every action to God. According to Romans 8:5-8, an un-renewed mind leaves a Believer in limbo because the focus of the mind submits the body to what it serves. Until a man's mind is renewed he is subject to many shifts.

*For they that are after the flesh do **mind** the things of the flesh;*
but they that are after the Spirit the things of the Spirit.
*For to be **carnally minded** is death; but to be **spiritually minded** is life*
and peace. Because the carnal mind is enmity against God:
for it is not subject to the law of God, neither indeed can be.

So then they are in the flesh cannot please God.

As I draw a contrast between the two kinds of life, notice, that there is a life dominated by sinful human nature, whose focus and center is self. There is a life dominated by the Spirit of God, that is **Spirit controlled** and **Christ dominated**. These two lives are going in diametrically opposite directions. The first is pointed daily towards death; the latter is steadily progressing towards God each day. Like Enoch who walked with God and God took him. God's will is that man has the mind of Christ.

Let this mind be in you, which was also in Christ Jesus: who being in the form of God, thought it not robbery to be equal with God:
(Philippians 2:5, 6, KJV)

In closer examination of 1 Corinthians 9.25-27, the Apostle Paul emphatically states the importance of self-control in striving for mastery. He urges the Believer to develop the fruit of *temperance* in all things.

*"And every man that strives for the mastery is **temperate** in all things. Now they do it to obtain a corruptible crown but we are incorruptible.*

I have already discussed how athletes who pursue natural crowns and accomplishments will do whatever it takes to become achievers. This selective group of aspiring men and women willingly forsake family, natural pleasures, and many other daily distractions for the sake of obtaining a gold medal.

Several years ago in desperate pursuit of the gold medal, young figure skater, Tanya Harding injured another contestant, Nancy Kerrigan, who was projected to win the gold. Even though this rare example illustrates how the wrong focus on competing generates a lack of focus on personal development and preparation. Tanya's inability to structure and focus on the goal at hand forced her to resort to unthinkable measures to win the gold. Instead of putting her best foot forward, she tried eliminating her competitor instead of applying determination, preparation, and discipline. However, there are heaps of heroic Olympic stories demonstrating triumph and victory reflecting the *"power of temperance."*

Paul said, they do it (self-discipline, temper) to obtain a corruptible crown but, we must do it to receive an incorruptible crown. God promises that each of us, who will diligently prepare ourselves through faith, to trust in Him with all our hearts, in spite of what we must overcome, will receive the favor and goodness of the Lord. That is why Believers should spend time each day ensuring that all of their practices, systems, and operations are structured according to God's Word.

The seven components listed below, if applied consistently, enables Believers to experience godliness resulting in wholesome and successful living. These components establish the spirit as the dominant part of man.

The Seven Components to Structure

1. Pray Always (ask, supplicate, intercede, give thanks)

2. Seek the Kingdom's way first (study, meditate on Scriptures)

3. Walk in Love (imitate Christ's character, obey commands, believe that God's way is best)

4. Walk by Faith (trust God's Word in all things)

5. Walk in the Spirit (obey God's Word despite difficulty)

6. Live in Self-denial (avoid offense, exalt others, reckon yourself "dead to self" but "alive in Him")

7. Be fruitful (commit to live as a fruitful godly character to win souls)

I'M PRAYING FOR YOUR DISCOVERY

As we continue to explore 1 Corinthians 9:25-27, concentrating on *temperance* as the focal point, I pray you begin to recognize and accept God's will and purpose for your life. There is tremendous fulfillment in purposeful, goal-driven living. Paul says that athletes and competitors have goals, aspirations, and chief aims that are worth buffeting their bodies and forsaking many loved ones. Jesus said that when a man truly loves Him he will *"forsake all to follow him."* It's amazing how people are simply not effective because they don't have a chief aim or definite purpose in life that is aligned with God's word.

Those who discover the need for purpose have something to conform to and structure their lives around. Without a chief aim or a central purpose you become subject to defeat and confusion frequently. Those with a chief aim shoot at specific targets. They are never satisfied hitting the things around the target. Nothing, but the bull's-eye, which is their chief aim, will satisfy them.

This is another reason so many persons struggle day-after-day with keeping devotional periods and daily reading consistent Bible study and confessions of Scripture that generate faith and develop character. This is simply because of the absence of a chief aim or a defined purpose. Jesus said, *"If you love me you will keep my commandments."* The right emotion and thought (which is love) will generate the right action in response to the right information.

The developing of plans, ideas, and concepts successfully requires continuity of thought and passionate desire that generates strong focus combined with a commitment to constant application. For example, an artist progresses as far as time permits each day, until the ideas captivated in the photo-static membrane of his or her mind are fully depicted upon the canvas.

The Process

THOUGHT: As an artist, I begin with the end in mind, the place where all plans must begin. Thought and imagination are the functions of the mind that gives us the ability to see the end or final result of a thing. The only true place that allows an individual to accurately plot the steps of accomplishment is his mind. "His mind must conceive it and believe it, if he is to achieve it."

PLAN: He selects the tools necessary to accomplish his desire and organizes them. Then he estimates the amount of time needed, prepares the canvas, mixes the colors and sets the time to begin.

ACTION: His burning desire to portray the image that is so indelibly imprinted on his mind is the driving force that interlinks his thoughts and talents from day-to-day until he sees his desire accomplished.

Day after day, the artist's **goal**, which is the image *inside* of him, *ignites* passion and desire which *motivates his attitude*, and *stimulates* his *talent* into manipulating and creating contour and color, depth and light and collages and forms that draw him closer to completion each day.

In spite of distractions, problems that may arise, or even setbacks, his ability to stay focused on the image inside will enable him to persevere unto completion.

Here are three tips that will assist you in accomplishing your God-given, word-tested desires.

1. **Thoughtcontinuity**andconnectionfromday-to-daylinksyourideas and concepts together.

2. **Too many breaks** will cause you to lose sight of what you are developing. This may result in frustration and confusion and make it a challenge to restart or know where to begin again. Allowing too many breaks between starting and completing can lead to failure.

3. Anyone attempting to climb, risk the possibility of a fall but to exist in an environment where there is no attempt is to exist where falling

is inevitable and becomes common practice. This is unacceptable! Expect obstacles.

Air Beaters

Now, who actually beats at the air? Simply put, people who do what they do without the proper components of duty are those who beat at the air. Duty must be present in order to sustain the passion and motivation needed to accomplish the underlined objective. Don't just swing for the sake of swinging; stop showing up at church on Sunday just for the sake of being there. Refuse to sing in the choir just to show how good you are!

Listen, bad and anointed are distinctly different. A person who has a chief aim, commitment, and desire to work for the Lord to further His cause and purpose usually loves the work they do and are "joy generators." These are the ones that God will anoint. But those who neglect to search for deeper purposes than association and occupancy (those who perform without defined purpose) will work as hard, if not harder, without fulfillment and without anointing.

Example

I will never forget the many experiences of my teen years in various choirs and the teaching ministry that allowed me to witness how time, temptation, and trouble would always test and determine the type of people we were partnering with. These types of people are usually singing just to be singing in the choir. Yet they never transfer the songs or the motivation of the song into their personal lives. In a short period of time they might experience a loss of excitement, run out of fuel, and eventually deteriorate in their commitment leading them into sporadic attendance prior to quitting. We *all* need a sense of purpose about why we do what we do. We also need a chief aim. Chief aims enable us to focus regardless of the distractions that are sure to come.

A meaningful struggle in context

Why is it so hard for individuals to structure their lives? It's difficult because those individuals have lived without structure for so long. It's very hard for dysfunctional individuals to manifest a reality externally that they have never envisioned or imagined internally. It's also very difficult for people to commit to a transitional lifestyle when it has never been a part of their daily routine.

Most of us adapt to things that don't require much change rather smoothly. It's easier to get involved in something that is similar to what you are already apart of, even though, in many cases this too is a hard task. The key here is that we need a chief aim, a goal that gives us purpose. If we never establish a definite purpose we will never have a reason to structure our lives. It really should be difficult for anyone to settle for mere existence. That's mediocrity!

Psalms 1:1-3 list five basic steps that are structured to manifest prosperity in the lives of Believers who conform to its simplified demands.

*Blessed is the man that ***walketh** not in the counsel of the ungodly,*

nor *standeth in the way of the sinners, nor *sitteth in the seat
of the scornful. But his *delight is in the law of the Lord:
and in his law doth he *meditate day and night. And he shall be like
a tree planted by the rivers of water, that bringeth forth his fruit in his
season; his leaf also shall not wither;
and whatsoever he doeth shall prosper. (Psalm 1:1-3)

Notice that this is not a quick fix but a process that must be walked out through time. Life is a process, not an event. Those who really need immediate or swift results wear out fast, or they burn out quick. Since they think they need to see physical or material evidence before they get started, they are usually very easily discouraged.

While each of the five steps are important, step one is the most pivotal step. Step one reflects the necessity of steps four and five. Let's call these steps "the structured lifestyle of the blessed."

Structured Lifestyle of the Blessed:

Step 1. Does not seek or accept ungodly counsel (advice, information)

Step 2. Does not stand where sinners stand

Step 3. Does not sit in scorn

Step 4. His delights and desires are in the law of God

Step 5. He meditates in that law day and night

A recovering addict once commented "I went to church every Wednesday and every Sunday for a solid month and nothing happen. I'll be honest with you; I gave it my all, so I'm not going back. If God was going to do anything for me he would have done it then, because I was more faithful then than I have ever been in all my life. In fact, I didn't sin for that month; I told no lies, I paid all my bills, and I did not try any of my former habits that month. You think God cared? No, not at all! God did nothing to help me."

For this reason the Bible teaches that, *"in your patience you possess your soul."* Hebrews 10:36 states *"for you have need of patience, that after you have done the will of God, ye might receive the promise."* Today's society has progressed into a quick fix; hurry up, fast-food system that serves up the product of desire without the proper ingredients needed to sustain the good produced.

The cost is premium, but the quality is poor. Seemingly, these type entities have nurtured the idea that life is an event where one miracle will happen and everyone will ride off into the sunset, healthy, wealthy, and wise. Life is not an event. Life is a process! This process requires focus, diligence, knowledge, wisdom, hard work and many other virtues that bring peace and wholesomeness. What we must realize is that the spirit-man prioritizes life totally different than the soul and physical-man (natural) man does. Remember, man is a *tripartite* or (three-part being). What makes man effective is when there is an emergence between all three personalities (spirit, soul, and body) based upon godly or spiritual reasoning while the spirit man is the controller.

What makes man a negative presence that works against himself that his body or (natural-man) is dominated by worldly information and merges with his soul-man without the priority of the spirit-man empowered by Kingdom or spiritual knowledge and wisdom? Realize that whomever the soul-man merges with (between natural and spiritual) becomes the dominant expression and reigning chief of our being.

Some people have no sense of purpose because the appetite of their body determines every place they go and everything they do. For instance, they leave the Sunday worship service without devising a system that will enable reflection on the message preached. So, in desperation they need a meal, a smoke, some form of entertainment, or fellowship immediately. This is an early indication that their body is in control of their soul and therefore ruling the whole man.

This practice silences the spirit part of your triune man and rules the whole man. The silencing of the spirit part of your tri-unity subjects the whole man to hardship, stresses, and many unnecessary exchanges that could be avoided.

So what you have to do is learn how to prioritize life through the filters of the spirit-man. This begins with proper **Hearing** which I will address later. But in this case my emphasis is to properly discern. In Mark 4:23-34, Jesus said, *"If any man has ears to hear, let him hear. And he said unto them, take heed what you hear."* In other words, what or whom you listen to can seriously determine your success or failure.

The Power of Advice

Note in Psalms 1:1 that the word **counsel** there means **advice**. *"Blessed is the man who walketh not in the counsel of the ungodly."* The Amplified says, *"Blessed happy, fortune, prosperous and enjoyable is the man who walks and lives not in the counsel of the ungodly."*

In other words, to follow ungodly advice, to follow their plans, or to follow their purposes is tragic. But, godly advice is profitable and necessary in all things, and at all times.

During the early months of summer I noticed that I had actually slipped back into a pattern of attracting time wasters and distracters that were causing me great frustrations because I was being hindered from completing important tasks. One morning while praying, the Holy Spirit directed me to visit a good friend who lives a very structured and highly productive life. I left church immediately to solicit his assessment of my situation. As I entered his store I observed him very cautiously moving across the floor aware of his customers but focused on finishing his task.

"Hi Bro!" I said, reluctantly, (not wanting to impose). "I need your input on something briefly if you can spare a few minutes." "Sure," He replied. We entered his office and sat down, and I began laying out my frustrations. Looking straight into my eyes as an intense physician would, he replied! "Pastor Bush, **your value is determined by the amount of problems you solve for others, not by how many people you listen to.** In your position as the senior leader of the church the majority of your time must not be spent on the least priorities or small fires that subordinates can resolve, because **people, who don't respect your time, won't respect your wisdom!**" Although, He shared many other prudent tips that day, these two highlighted statements helped me to initiate changes that enabled me to become more effective and get back on track.

Notice, after clarifying the power of advice the Psalmist continues; *"Nor stands submissive and inactive in the path where sinner walk, nor* *sits down to relax and rest where the scornful and the mockers gather; but **his delight and desire** are in the law of the Lord and on his law the precepts, the instructions, the teachings of God he habitually meditates, (he ponders and studies) by day and by night and **he shall be like a tree firmly planted** by and tended by the streams of water ready to bring forth his fruits in its season, his leaf also shall not fade or wither and **everything he does** shall prosper."*

I can't promise you prosperity any other way, but God's way. We are blessed if we refuse to walk in the counsel of the ungodly. Now, the Word of God distinctly tells us how we should eat, it tells us the proper way to rest, the proper way to manage money, the proper way to maintain health, what our relationships ought to look like, how we should conduct ourselves on the job, how our marriages should be structured, and how Kingdom parenting should be conducted.

It tells us when and how to purchase, how to build a house, how to redeem our time, and how to walk in the spirit. It tells us everything we need to know in order to be effective in gathering Kingdom inheritance in our earthly life. In fact Proverbs 4.26 implies that there is an established route for success in every endeavor. *"Ponder the path of thy feet, and let all thy ways be established."* (KJV)

Another view of Psalms 1:1 is that the most ungodly advice you will hear will come from within you! Nobody will talk to you about doing the evil, selfish, foolish, insensitive, sinful, hurtful, harmful, lustful, and wicked deeds that you will do like Satan and your untrained "self".

Most people are afraid to tell you to go and get sloppy drunk and make a fool of yourself. The majority certainly would not dare tell you to rob a bank. Regardless of how a person may feel or think about you, most would not assume the liberty to suggest extreme activities unless you are partners in some type of conspiracy or plan together. It's true! We as humans give ourselves some very wicked counsel.

HOW INFORMATION GETS IN THE MIX

Believers and non-believers must realize that the problem is not we, it's me! The problem isn't what others say to us, it is what we say to ourselves after we hear it. What God is trying to convey through the psalmist is that our ungodly nature gets the best of us when empowered by ungodly counsel. Ungodly counsel (words we hear) both internal and external are destructive forces. Dr. Myles Munroe once stated that *"wisdom protects us from the dangers of knowledge."* Certainly, we need the wisdom of God as a filter for all incoming information.

When we listen to ungodly counsel, we fuel the ungodly part of our tripartite which is considered fleshly or carnal. When we listen to godly counsel we fuel our spirit part. The abundance of what we listen to actually develops or determines the functions and reasoning of our soul part. This ultimately influences the activities and responses of our body.

When information influences our thoughts and emotions, if it is allowed to reside while compounding with similar sorts, it will determine the posture (will or attitude) of the *soul part* of our tri-unity. The Apostle Paul says in Romans 8:5 that **the fixed state of our mind**

will determine the course of our walk. *"For they that are after the flesh do mind the things of the flesh; but they that are after the Spirit the things of the Spirit."*

In the Gospel of Matthew 12:34-35 Jesus said, *"From the abundance of the heart the mouth speaks* (is influenced)." (KJV) The Amplified states, *"For out of the fullness, the overflow, the superabundance of the heart the mouth speaks. The good man from his **inner good treasure** flings forth good things, and the evil man out of his **inner evil store house** flings forth evil things. Notice, the implication here is that life does not just happen to us, but our quality of living comes from within us.*

The Apostle also warned the Corinthians of the danger of receiving from improper sources; "Do not be so deceived and misled! Evil companionships, (communion, associations) corrupt and deprave good manners and morals and character." (1Corinthians 15:33, AMP)

Clearly these scriptures enable us to understand why the Holy Spirit impressed upon the psalmist the steps necessary to empower the spirit-man as the reigning chief of the triune man and establish the heart (soul) in the Kingdom of God system.

My Rule of Thumb
Things to remember regarding the use of each "structure" ingredient.

1.   Work out your own salvation by discovering the principles that will navigate you through prearranged paths that God made ready for us ahead of time that we should walk in them living according to his will. This process is called "laboring to enter into his rest".

2.   The Kingdom of God consist of straight gates and narrow ways that are designed to put new converts back in right relationship with God, which results in a life of rest and peace.

3.   Entering the Kingdom means to realign your life and its issues after receiving salvation (soteria), which initiates the deposit of abundant life.

4.   Realignment of issues requires "mind renewal." You must think differently to become different.

5.   Mind renewal requires prayerful Bible study, research, constant hearing, confessing the Word, daily meditating the Word, and pondering the path of your feet. Observing closely your conduct and relationships, so that your ways may progressively be reestablished to represent your Kingdom citizenship.

6.   Acknowledge that many of your ways (habits, beliefs, convictions, and responses) that seemed right continue to end in destruction, thus making your situations worst. These must be put on the hit list for change!

7.   **Accepting that if your present established beliefs, habits, and responses to a particular issue do not yield peace, joy, and righteousness combined to produce wholesome living, your approach or practice regarding that issue is not producing God's best.**

8.   God's righteousness through Scriptures is designed to reprove, correct, and instruct you into His perfect will to secure for you a well-balanced and wholesome life.

9.   Remember God's thoughts and ways are not like ours, but He gave

us His word and His Spirit to bridge the gap and give us rest.

10. Your best example is Jesus; the expressed image of God.

"He always did those things that pleased the father." God wants each of us to gain mastery over ourselves through Kingdom principles which are designed to enlighten and empower successful living in every area of our lives. Remember you have the Holy Spirit living inside of you to help and guide you daily.

In the Kingdom of God the roads have been mapped out and the way paved, so I invite you to take this adventurous journey by using these ingredients of structure and your life will become more purposeful and fulfilling each day!

EIGHT INGREDIENTS OF "STRUCTURE"

Volume 1

My **VISION** needs TRANSCRIPTION

My **TIME** needs an ASSIGNMENT

My **RELATIONSHIPS** need DEFINING

My **MONEY** needs a MISSION

My **FAITH** needs a DEFINITE GOAL and a CHIEF AIM

My **CONFESSIONS** need RESTRICTIONS

My **THOUGHTS** need to be TRIED

My **EMOTIONS** need to be WEIGHED

CHAPTER
7

THE USE OF LAWS AND PRINCIPLES

Remember that as you journey, your regard and honor for principles must be heighten to a level that allows you to always know that Laws and principles have no greater respect for a crawling infant or toddler just beginning to walk than for a senior citizen turning one-hundred-years-old.

If either were actually taken to a sixteen story roof and allowed to wonder beyond the edge, they would experience a deadening fall that would probably be regarded as something God allowed or simply something God planned. But neither explanation would stand up against the truth.

Truth is the laws and principles that govern life do not respect the ignorant, intelligent, or disobedient, no more than the obedient, unless they adhere to their existence. Ignorance of the laws and principles does not change their demands. I have yet to see the law of gravity change its nature to respect any force weaker than itself.

Only when a higher law is initiated, does the reigning law yield!

As in the case of the law of gravity which is always a force to reckon with in the earth-realm versus the law of thrust. Even though, what goes up must come down, whenever the rate of speed is accomplished within an accelerated span of time, the law of thrust super seeds the law of gravity because gravity now yields to it.

In order for you to overcome the way of fleshly nature you must walk in the spirit. This is clearly what the apostle Paul meant in Romans 8:2, 3, *"For the law of the Spirit of life in Christ Jesus has made me free from the law of sin and death. For what the law could not do in that it was weak through the flesh, God did by sending His own Son in the likeness of sinful flesh, on account of sin: He condemned sin in the flesh, that the righteous requirement of the law might be fulfilled in us who do not walk according to the flesh but according to the Spirit." Here James also states "It is not the hearers of the law that are just before God, but the doers who shall be justified."*

LET'S GET CONSCIOUS ABOUT SETTING OUR ATTITUDE RIGHT ONCE AND FOR ALL

The time has come when we can no longer afford to have conflicting feelings about our response to foundational things. The feeling of ambivalence has dominated the operation of many confused, disinterested, and ignorant Believers resulting in the appearance of "brokenness without remedy."

The Demand forStructured Discipline

It is the difference between *the hard and the easy way.* There is never an "easy way" to greatness; greatness is always the product of toil. Hesiod, the old Greek poet, writes, "Wickedness can be had in abundance easily; smooth is the road, and very nigh she dwells; but in front of virtue the gods immortal have put sweat." Epicharmus said, "The gods demand of us toil as the price of all good things." "Knave," he warns, "Yearn not for the soft things, lest thou earn the hard."

William Barkley gives this account in his Bible commentary on what it takes to develop discipline for success: "Once, Edmund Burke made a great speech in the House of Commons. Afterwards his brother Richard Burke was observed in deep thought. He was asked what he was thinking about, and answered, "I have been wondering how it has come about that Ned has contrived to monopolize all the talents of our family; but then again I remember that **when we were at play, he was always at work.**"

Even when a thing is done with an appearance of ease, that ease is the product of unremitting toil. The skill of the master executants on the piano, or the champion player on the golf course did not come without sweat. There never has been any other way to greatness than the way of toil, and anything else which promises such a way is a delusion and a snare.

It is the difference between *the disciplined and the undisciplined way. Nothing was ever achieved without discipline;* and many an athlete and **many a man has been ruined because he abandoned discipline**

and let himself grow slack. Coleridge is the supreme tragedy of his indiscipline. Never did so great a mind, produce so little.

He left Cambridge University to join the army; he left the army because, in spite of all his erudition, he could not rub down a horse; he returned to Oxford and left without a degree. He began a paper called *The Watchman* which lived for ten numbers (100 years) and then died. It has been said of him: "He lost himself in *visions of work to be done,* that always remained to be done. Coleridge had every poetic gift but one-the gift of sustained and concentrated effort."

In his head and in his mind he had all kinds of books, as he said, himself, "completed save for transcription." "I am on the eve, "he says, "of sending to the press two octavo volumes." **But the books were never composed outside Coleridge's mind; because he would not face the *discipline* of sitting down to write them out.** No one ever reached any eminence, and no one having reached it ever maintained it, **without discipline."** (Barklay)

THE IMPORTANCE OF STRUCTURED DISCIPLINES

Proverbs 16:32, *He that is slow to anger is better than the mighty; and he that ruleth his spirit than he that taketh a city.*

Here wisdom has determined it as vitally necessary for the twenty-first century Kingdom citizen to have the grace of meekness and self-discipline. Grace that will assist all Believers in learning important lessons, navigating their course successfully, and in making proper adjustments during these difficult times that are now upon us.

To effectively communicate the importance of today's Believers developing consistent character, I chose this passage because here, a person's priority is to be *slow to anger*, not easily offended, put into passion, nor apt to resent provocation. But he or she must take time to consider before engaging others with-out-of-control outbreaks.

This tempered citizen is so slow in their motions towards anger that they may be quickly stopped and put to ease. One who "rules" as if in control of every increment on the scale of their character may respond appropriately.

It is to have the rule of **our own spirits, appetites,** affections, and all our **inclinations**, but particularly our **passions**, and **anger**, keeping them under direction and check.

In other words, as Christians we are to rule or be lords over our anger as God demonstrates throughout the Scriptures. We must be *lords of our anger*, as God is, spoken of in Nahum 1:3, Notice, *"The Lord is slow to anger, and great in power."* Ephesians 4:26, admonishes that we *"Be angry and sin not."*

Next, notice the honor of such meekness. He that gets and keeps the mastery of his passions *is better than the mighty, better than he that takes a city.* Such a person is acknowledged as greater than Alexander or Ce´sar who were both responsible for great conquest.

The conquest of self and our own unruly passions require more true wisdom and a more steady, constant, and regular management than obtaining a victory over the forces of an enemy or controlling the lives of others.

We who are slow to anger understand that to represent God means to demonstrate only His character in times of testing: *"When a man's ways please the LORD, He makes even his enemies to be at peace with him."* (Proverbs 16:7)

Believer's who are Slow to Anger are far better than the Mighty

A second mention of this quality that speaks mainly to the disadvantage of undisciplined living is also found in Proverbs 25:28, **"He that *hath* no rule over his own spirit *is like* a city that is broken down, *and* without walls."**

While the person that has *rule over his own spirit* maintains the government of himself, and of his own appetites and passions, he does not suffer them to rebel against reason and conscience. He has the rule of his own thoughts, his desires, his inclinations, his resentments, and keeps them all in order. He learns wisely how to interact with others by examining closely the difficult challenge of managing himself.

In contrast the man who has no rule over his own spirit who, when temptations are before him, has no government of himself. When he is offended or provoked he breaks out into unrestrained, misguided passions, which causes him to appear *"like a city that is broken down and without walls."*

His failure to prioritize the development of systems and methods to assist him in ruling himself, have left him exposed to the temptations of Satan. Such a person becomes an easy prey to that diabolical enemy who constantly brings assaults against his assignment, leaving him liable to many troubles and vexations.

Years ago, I had to acknowledge as a leader that attempting to reconstruct a life is a very difficult challenge. Many times we focus on the secondary rather than the primary. Leading others is secondary, leading ourselves is primary.

I desperately needed to go through the process of gaining mastery over my own personal struggles if I was to succeed in assisting others with their struggles. Like the Apostle Paul, I had to learn how to *"keep my body disciplined, to bring it into subjection; for fear that after proclaiming the things pertaining to the gospel to others. I myself should become unfit, and be rejected as a counterfeit."*

Constant introspection and self honesty enabled me to realize that God provides leadership for us by the Holy Spirit. However, it is our responsibility to use His Word to train and discipline ourselves to remain fit to be led as His witnesses.

Jesus promised in the gospel of John 8:32-33,

"Then Jesus said to those Jews who believed Him,

*"If you abide in My word, you are My **disciples** indeed.*

And you shall know the truth,

and the truth shall make you free."

Friends there are hundreds of "if's" in the Bible which are conditional and require specific responses in order to enjoy its benefits. This is a primary reason to start exercising and practicing His righteousness today. Even the Apostle Paul acknowledges that to live without discipline frustrates the empowerment of the Holy Spirit.

STRIVING FOR A CROWN

"Do you not know that those who run in a race all run, but one receives the prize? **Run in such a way that you may obtain it.** *And everyone who competes for the prize is* **temperate in all things.** *Now they do it to obtain a perishable crown, but we for an imperishable crown. Therefore I run thus: not with uncertainty. Thus I fight: not as one who beats the air. But* **I discipline my body** *and bring it into subjection, lest, when I have preached to others, I myself should become disqualified."* (1 Corinthians 9:24-28, NKJV)

YOU must UNDERSTAND the importance of "VISION"

"Where there is no vision [no redemptive revelation of God], the people perish; but he who keeps the law [of God, which includes that of man]--blessed (happy, fortunate, and enviable) is he."

CHAPTER

8

MY VISION NEEDS TRANSCRIPTION

Then the LORD answered me and said: *"Write the vision and make it plain on tablets, that he may run who reads it.* For the vision is yet for an appointed time; But at the end it will speak, and it will not lie. Though it tarries, wait for it; because it will surely come, it will not tarry. "Behold the proud, His soul is not upright in him; But the just shall live by his faith. Hab. 2:2-4

Clearly the emphasis of Proverbs 29:18 suggests that any person, family, group, organization, government system, or society that is without "vision" is destined to perish.

Vision must serve as the **internal filtration device** through which you use to make pertinent decisions, determine your priorities, establish daily activities or necessary duties, and respond to all of your shifting circumstances and unanticipated challenges on a regular basis.

It also acts as a default mechanism that enables you to consistently decide what will impact the flow of your life and ability so you are always able to continue mounting progress.

In other words, vision will help you be specific about the type of persons, activities, habits, environments, rest and diet along with other significant functions that should be a part of your life. This is the primary reason I refer to vision as **the Cornerstone to a prosperous life.** It is as Webster's New World Dictionary defined it; the basic, essential, or most important part of the foundation.

THE CORNERSTONE TO A PROSPEROUS LIFE

In the Gospel of Matthew 7:24-27 Jesus said, *"These words I speak to you are not incidental additions to your life, homeowner improvements to your standard of living. They are foundational words, words to build a life on. If you work these words into your life, you are like a smart carpenter who built his **house on solid rock.** Rain poured down, the river flooded, a tornado hit—but nothing moved that house. It was fixed to the rock.*

"But if you just use my words in Bible studies and don't work them into your life, you are like a stupid carpenter who built his house on the sandy beach. When a storm rolled in and the waves came up, it collapsed like a house of cards."

Again in Matthew 12:13-17, *"Now when Jesus went into the region of Caesarea Philippi, He asked His disciples, Who do people say that the Son of Man is? And they answered, some say John the Baptist; others say Elijah; and others Jeremiah or one of the prophets. He said to them, but who do you [yourselves] say that I am? Simon Peter replied, you are the Christ, the Son of the living God.*

*Then Jesus answered him, Blessed (happy, fortunate, and to be envied) are you, Simon Bar-Jonah. For flesh and blood [men] have not **revealed** this to you, but My Father Who is in heaven. And I tell you, you are Peter [Greek, Petros--a large piece of rock], and **on this rock** [Greek, petra—a huge rock like Gibraltar] I will build My church, and the gates of Hades (the powers of the infernal region) shall not overpower it [or be strong to its detriment or hold out against it]. I will give you the keys of the kingdom of heaven; and whatever you bind (declare to be improper and unlawful) on earth must be what is already bound in heaven; and whatever you loose (declare lawful) on earth must be what is already loosed in heaven.*

It is clear from the teaching of scriptures that Jesus the son of God who died for the sins of the world is the Chief-corner stone to life. But to progress in life as a wholesomely fulfilled individual either naturally or spiritually requires sight (natural) or faith (spiritual). Here faith must become to your spirit-man what your eyes are to your natural-man. *"For we walk by faith [we regulate our lives and conduct ourselves by our conviction or belief respecting man's relationship to God and divine things, with trust and holy fervor; thus we walk] not by sight or appearance."* 2 Cor. 5:7Amp

As children of God we are given the opportunity to **"Live an Expectation Driven Reality!"** But we must refuse to have *sight* without *vision!* Sight is the limited function of your lower nature; vision is the eye of faith (spiritual sight) that gives it immediate substance to God appointed realities. Without vision faith is blind and stagnant because it has no object to hope for or nothing to look forward to.

God appointed realities are offspring's of prophecies, promises, or merely words from God that when revealed to us birth desire or aspirations that cause us to hunger for their attainment or manifestation. This is "righteous hunger" the kind of hunger Jesus said it is a blessing to have. But as you acquire this hunger you must be swift to write it down (record it) and make it plain for your pursuit.

In John 12:16 of The Message states *"The disciples didn't notice the fulfillment of many Scriptures at the time, but after Jesus was glorified, they remembered that what was written about him matched what was done to him."* Notice how the Scripture identified his strict adherence and conformance to what was written about Him.

Now let's compare this account with His address to Peter in verses 36-38. *"Simon Peter asked, "Master, just where are you going?" Jesus answered, "You can't now follow me where I'm going. You will follow later. Master," said Peter, "why can't I follow now? I'll lay down my life for you! Really? You'll lay down your life for me?* **The truth is that before the rooster crows, you'll deny me three times."** These two accounts enable us to see that there is a difference in seeing and knowing, or looking and seeing. Dr. Myles Monroe once said, "Many look but few see".

True God inspired vision demands that we live an expectation-driven reality. Keep in mind that, there are **two realities** that make up **life**; the one **you see** and the one **God says**. The first is **natural [limited]**, the latter is **spiritual [unlimited]**. Vision is born from **God's supernatural words** called **"Truth"** which is the **"ultimate reality"**.

Through vision you see tomorrow today! First, your beliefs must be based upon the **Word of faith** not what you see or sense. Because if you continue to base your beliefs on sense knowledge, eventually everything becomes a problem and a threat to the security spiritual stability as Believers. Many Believers who fail to make this transition continue to walk by sight and live offended lives with good reasons.

Next, you must realize that sight usually relates to a thing according to its appearance, vision-filled faith relates to things as God intended them to be. This is why we must meditate and spend time with God.

Through meditation or muttering the mind is given the opportunity to handle words until they are transmuted into pictures. Since we see in pictures, we gain concept when we are able to change a feeling or a word into a thought or image.

The more time we spend with this exchange the more intense our passion for its reality becomes. Thus the image progresses into an imagination and from this a motion picture is born within us that now houses a procedural grace which makes what was difficult to accomplish or attain now an easy transition. Now, the reality is indelibly imprinted on the internal canvas of your mind. **You must write your "vision" down!**

Until you transcribe your vision so that you can see it on paper and begin laboring with it daily to develop a relationship with it, what you desire will be meaningless in your daily pursuits. When we can see through *spiritual vision*, better than our *natural senses* then we can prove through mind *transformation* what the *perfect will of GOD* is. This is why Paul said it is urgent that we renew our minds in Romans 12:1, 2.

I arrived at this point after many years of allowing either Satan or my ignorance to lead me into accepting good people, good things, and mediocre situations over a great life. Today, I live a great life, a life of purpose, peace, and daily fulfillment. Yesterday, even though I was genuinely born again, my life had no distinct purpose, no real direction, no continuity or flow.

As I'll describe later in each of the structured disciplines that became inclusive ingredients in the reconstructing of my new life, I was very active, busy, and helpful but not fulfilled. While making this acknowledgment of my own personal misery, the Holy Spirit said to me *"the absence of vision driven by corresponding action is the reason many people are miserable"*.

I had to learn that I was categorically a "busy-procrastinator" who like so many others was deceived by my own heart. The way to true life is straight and narrow; few are they who find it. It is a life that one must press to enter because of the many adversaries that are cosmic, self-made, and decision driven. Vision is a daring call to be different because it demands that you conform to your unique design and God-given purpose.

It is a well-spring to life from which all other meaningful and purposeful activity flows. Years ago, during my first ten years of Pastoral ministry leading as a pastor was relatively easy for me. I had good people skills and very high tolerance for almost everyone that came into the ministry. Growth was also easy because the primary focus was love and acceptance without demand for change.

But, eventually I grew weary of this type of climate because I found myself catering to demands that did not match the demands and convictions that God had placed upon my life. These were the things and the original purpose that I knew God had called me to fulfill.

As time progressed I grew to where non-functioning leaders and position holders who seemed to relish "titles" but not satisfy their positional demands could not be tolerated at all. In fact I developed a "no tolerance" agitation for those who were aware of their deficiency but did nothing to change or grow to conform to positional expectations.

Matthew 15:14 and 23:16-26 (NKJV) gave me the insight that reinforced my decision because it made me aware of how "blind guides or blind leaders" who held prominent positions that require vision frustrated Jesus.

*"Let them alone. They are **blind leaders** of the blind. And **if the blind leads the blind,** both will fall into a ditch."*

*"Woe to you, **blind guides**, who say, Whoever swears by the temple, it is nothing; but whoever swears by the gold of the temple, he is obliged to perform it. **Fools and blind!** For which is greater, the gold or the temple that sanctifies the gold? And, 'Whoever swears by the altar, it is nothing; but whoever swears by the gift that is on it, he is obliged to perform it. **Fools and blind!** For which is greater, the gift or the altar that sanctifies the gift? Therefore he who swears by the altar, swears by it and by all things on it. He who swears by the temple, swears by it and by Him who dwells in it. And he who swears by heaven, swears by the throne of God and by Him who sits on it. Woe to you, scribes and Pharisees, hypocrites! For you pay tithe of mint and anise and cummin, and have neglected the weightier matters of the law: justice and mercy and faith. These you ought to have done, without leaving the others undone. **Blind guides**, who strain out a gnat and swallow a*

*camel! Woe to you, scribes and Pharisees, hypocrites! For you cleanse the outside of the cup and dish, but inside they are full of extortion and self-indulgence. **Blind Pharisee**, first cleanse the inside of the cup and dish, that the outside of them may be clean also."*

Over and over, again and again, I would constantly hear a voice echo inside of me trying to convince me that even though all men may be good, all good men are not good for me and the vision God has purposed me to fulfill. So, the vision became the force behind all major decisions pertaining to leaders and positional gifts especially, because it demanded conformance-based performance over insignificant performance and activity.

Let's define the two words that carry the weight of Proverbs 29:18 **vision** and **perish**. **Vision** according to Webster is something supernaturally revealed. To paraphrase, it is *a revelation from God or a God implanted mental reality that houses the inborn purposes and plans* for an individual, family, church, or nation. It is the future exposed— *spiritually* in the mind today, before it manifests naturally tomorrow. Vision restrains, governs, and guides the operation perimeters of those to be impacted by it like a blueprint or a road map.

Therefore it must be written very plain and simple so everyone involved or to be impacted by it can understand how to purposefully conform their efforts and participation. Notice in Jeremiah 29:11 and Ephesians 2:10 of the Amplified Bible: **To perish** means to be destroyed, ruined, or wiped out. So, if we put these two words together the meaning exposes vision as God's way of birthing, sustaining, and directing the world or an individual to prevent their destruction or ruin.

Even though most of us will spend sufficient time planning entertainment and vacations, far too few of us have considered the need to plan our destiny along with our most precious resources: our gifts and our time.

- ✔ So what's the point?
- ✔ Do I have a destination in mind for my life?
- ✔ Have I plotted a strategy to get there?
- ✔ How will I know when I hit an important milestone or mark in my life?
- ✔ How will I know when I fall off course without vision or plans?
- ✔ Have I asked myself what I want to accomplish in my life? (Something to remember; most people do not monitor how they "spend" their time. But how you spend it determines what you purchase with it!)
- ✔ Ephesians 5:15 points out that time yields to us whatever we spend it on.
- ✔ What am I purchasing with my time?

  Here is what you must decide as you work through this book: If you spend your time on nothing, you will have nothing to show for it! If you spend your time on wrong things you will have wrong things to show for it! If you spend it on distractions, you will have distractions to show for it!

  But if you spend it on vision your future will emerge!
- ✔ Make every minute count! Remember to say to yourself: "I must first see, next plan, and then I must act, if I am going to live a purposeful life."

✔ Only action ignites my dreams, plans, and goals into a living force.

✔ Procrastination holds me back because of fear and insecurities.

✔ *To conquer fear I must learn to act without hesitation.

✔ *To act without hesitation requires strong familiarity with my plan.

What I have learned is that to operate by a God inspired, carefully planned vision is a solution that will affect every area of my life that has become a problem to me. This solution will integrate all the issues of your life into one so you can become the same person at home, work, and with friends. Remember, Jesus came that you might have abundant life.

"VISION-FILLED FAITH AND PURPOSEFUL OBEDIENCE TO GOD'S WORD"

By now you have heard me repeat many times, "for me the answer was structuring my life to align with the Word of God". This enabled me to always have a **standard** for my actions, a **guide** for directions, and **perimeters** to conform my actions and operations so that what I expect is the thing I manifest.

From this, the Holy Spirit inspired a principle using the acronym "EAM." The "E" is expectation, "A" is application, and the "M" is for manifestation. Everything I expect requires a specific application which ensures manifestation. This is how the integrity of God is affirmed. "He hastens to perform His word or He watches over his word to perform it", not the wrong interpretation of it.

What many lack is a vision or an **internal core** [commitment to the word] that allows you to define yourself, and then express that "defined self" in a way that makes life work for you. As long as you continue to allow yourself to be constantly **controlled by external forces** both your performance and well-being will continue to be severely affected.

Structured priorities affect us internally and externally. They affect the way we experience work and life, our relationships with others, and the degree in which we are successful in all our natural and spiritual pursuits. You must establish an internal core that corresponds with who you are by beginning to think through all of your exchanges relative to your internal core. It is true vision that keeps God at the center of an individual's life and as the primary reason we do what we do.

Your VISION must be TRANSCRIBED so your PURPOSE can be RATIFIED! Vision helps lay aside weight and sin. Through the power of vision my life has been transformed. These principle disciplines have worked together to help me structure and regain the purpose for my existence.

My **VISION** needed TRANSCRIPTION, My **TIME** needed an ASSIGNMENT, My **RELATIONSHIPS** needed DEFINING, My **MONEY** needed a MISSION, My **FAITH** needed a DEFINITE GOAL and a CHIEF AIM, My **CONFESSIONS** needed RESTRICTIONS, My **THOUGHTS** needed to be TRIED, My **EMOTIONS** needed to be WEIGHED.

CHAPTER
9

IT ALL BEGINS WITH TIME

How well do you understand that the use of your

TIME

Impacts your entire Life?

My Time Needs an Assignment!

"We are to make the very most of our time, buying up each opportunity, because the days are evil. Therefore do not be vague and thoughtless and foolish, but understanding and firmly grasping what the will of the Lord is." (Ephesians 5:16, 17)

The word of God makes a great deal out of order and priority. The Holy Spirit revealed to me at a very important time in my life that "when we live without priorities, we live out of order. When we live life out of order our life is in chaos. To avoid chaos we must learn to assign our time wisely and keep our appointments and corresponding commitments.

Paul's instructions to the brethren in Ephesus are specific and urgent, regarding the use of their time. Notice, the emphasis, *"Look carefully how you walk! Live purposefully and worthily and accurately, not as unwise and witless, but as wise, sensible and intelligent; making the very most of your time, buying up each opportunity, because the days are evil."*

In other words, maximize the use of every moment each day by wisely using every opportunity and assignment for the advancement of the purpose for which you were created. Indicating that time well spent equals the sure purchasing of a purposeful, worthy, accurate, wise, sensible, and intelligent life. The primary use of your "Time" should correspond with your vision and purpose each day.

He further instructs; *"Do not be vague and thoughtless and foolish, but understanding and firmly grasping what the will of the Lord is."*

This statement reaffirms the emphasis of the King James Version, which uses the phrase **"the circumspect walk."** A phrase that signifies **walking accurately**, and in the right way; in order to consistently walk in the way of God's will and intentional purpose for us. God's will for us, should always be first priority to us, because its' significant inclusion will determine both our life's peace and fulfillment.

"Not as fools", He implies, who strays away from their paths, enticed by all adventures, because they have no understanding of their duty, or the value of their souls. Their constant neglect, mental inactivity, and lack of proper personal maintenance, causes them to fall into sin, and destroy themselves by becoming captive to themselves and the will of Satan.

Clearly a quote from Miles Monroe, adequately describes the devastation of ignorance with regards to the abuse of time: "If you don't know the purpose of a thing, abuse is inevitable."

Time is possibly the single most abused, neglected, misappropriated, and unappreciated resource that all men share. This was certainly my case for many years because I really had no concept of time at all. Although similar to my ignorance of laws and principles that navigate success with money and relationships, I was totally, innocently blind to the laws and principles that govern successful time management.

I actually grew up thinking that it was appropriate to assist as many persons and situations as I possibly could. Hardly ever did I use the word "No." In fact for many years after I married my lovely wife and we were blessed with three beautiful kids. I wasted a lot of time in the streets after work, taking on task that concerned the welfare of others, cheating my family of their lawful needs that I was responsible for fulfilling as a husband and father.

I really thought I was doing what was required of me as a pastor, duplicating what I saw demonstrated by prominent area Pastors. Looking back, I'm amazed that my heart was able to deceive me into thinking that my duty as a Christian was to take care of everyone else's needs and God would automatically take care of mine.

I had absolutely no idea that I was using and abusing my "time" to violate "the laws of preservations". Even though I was very studious and fervent in prayer and meditation, I was deceived. Whether you call it, self-deceived, satanically-deceived, traditionally or religiously – deceived, or simply, young and dumb; However you wish to describe it, I was deceived.

Not only was I deceived but, the people who benefited from my self-deception, both young and old, let me stay that way; even though in many cases they were aware of the toll it was taking on my family life.

Categorically, I became a product of Paul's description of the zeal of Israel in his letter to the Romans, chapter 10:2-3, *"I bear them witness that they have a zeal and enthusiasm for God, but it is not enlightened and according to correct and vital knowledge. For being ignorant of the righteousness that God ascribes, which makes one acceptable to him in word, thought, and deed, and seeking to establish a righteousness, a means of salvation, of their own, they did not obey or submit themselves to God's righteousness."*

Looking back in retrospect, I'm amazed at how sincere, zealous, determined, consistently dependable, lovingly kind and liberally generous I was. I just couldn't stand to see people hungry, hurting and without. But I was wrong because I was using precious time to give away much of the financial resources and other blessings, privileges and opportunities that God was trying to extend to the four people I was most responsible for. This statement may come as a surprise to many, but I had to discover that **"Need does not move God, faith does!"**

Need is suppose to be used by those of us who represent God as an opportunity and a tool to teach, direct, and train others how to trust in "Jehovah God" who will both provide for them and show them the way of securing provisions for themselves. So they can also experience the fulfillment of the promise, *"And I will bless you to be* *a Blessing"*.

And like so many others who have not evaluated their religious (zealous) efforts against correct biblical righteousness, ignorance was slowly destroying me through my misaligned practices and perceived good deeds.

I never will forget the night I arrived home with my family in the car, after an awesome prayer meeting, and Bible study to discover that my lights or electricity was turned off, and I was broke! I mean "bur-r-r-roke!" Now, I'm saying it like this because at that time, even though I was in my twenties, my house note was only three-hundred-fifty dollars monthly. I had no water- bill; (my grocery, gas, and insurances) was less than seven-hundred-fifty dollars monthly combined. My salary at that time was over forty-thousand dollars annually. I did have a savings that I could not access, (probably the only reason it was safe), but otherwise, I was bur-r-r-roke! I was so broke that I couldn't afford the "o" to keep the "br" connected to the "ke", that's br-o-ke!

The problem was that I had taken off a half of my work shift earlier that day to transport someone to the hospital who had several children older than me. When I arrived at their home, I discovered that they did not have gas money, no grocery, nor had their mortgage note been paid, it was a few weeks over due.

Sensitive to the burden and heaviness, I thought God allowed me to discern, I volunteered to give part, but loan the rest of the money so the person would be relieved for surgery.

From this point the details get a little fuzzy, but I do remember arriving home just in time to pick up my wife and kids for Bible study.

The first question my wife asked me, as she got in the car, was did you pay the light-bill. My immediate reply was defensive, because I did not want her to know what I had done.

Her last words on the subject were, "I don't know why you are so defensive but I'm just letting you know they (Aiken-Electric) called and said if it's not paid today, the lights will be turned off." I said nothing else but tried to imply, all is well, I'll take care of it tomorrow.

But, I was in for a rude awakening. After returning home from this awesome Bible study, I alluded to earlier. The electricity was off. I went back outside to check the meter only to discover that the color of the tag had been changed without my consent.

I was trapped. I was angry, and I was caught. My wife refused to go with me to ask my parents for a loan to cover my irresponsibility.

So, there I was, the servant of God, whose entire day was spent running errands and providing for someone else in the name of God only to discover, that, God did not provide for my family, in the name of Finace. That really was a costly lesson.

The ride to my parents was long as I turned on the radio to FM 91.7. The teaching program was "Grace to You" featuring, Dr. John Macarthur. The lesson text was taken from 1 Timothy 5:8, *"if anyone does not provide for his own, and especially for those of his household, he has denied the faith and is worst than an unbeliever."* I had never heard such foolishness all my life, I thought wait a minute; this principle is actually in the Bible!

As I listen to his exposition, the point was clear that I was ignorant of many biblical principles of responsibility. I became deeply convicted and apologetic. My abuses of time, money, and relationships (family) were now evident to the point, it felt like sin. And from that experience till now, my life is subjected to Kingdom principles guided by the Holy Spirit.

I've learned that *"the way of man is not in him, to direct his steps" apart from the Spirit of God. But, "the steps of a good man are ordered by the Lord, He lighted his way."* Therefore, we should *"ponder the path of our feet and let all of our ways be established."* Not only did Hosea 4:6; ring loudly in my hearing, but, the words of Jesus to the Pharisees also ringed loudly. *"You search the scriptures, for in them you think you have eternal life; and these are they which testify of Me"* (John 5:39).

From that time until now, I have dedicated myself to study out Kingdom methods and practices before adopting them as personal practices. "Circumspect walking" is the effect of true wisdom because it enables Kingdom citizens to live and walk daily within the laws of correspondence while buying up every opportunity and maximizing the privilege of grace given to us.

It is also a metaphor taken from merchants and traders who diligently observe and improve the seasons for merchandise and trade. This insight demands that as Kingdom representatives we become great stewards of our time, because each of us is individually considered as a walking economy. **Everything we do in time is a direct response to the principle of "seed time and harvest or sowing and reaping".**

Again, the urgent emphasis of time redemption is to motivate you to buy back or to purchase your time so that you gain or regain ownership of enough of your time, to recover, to convert into, to set free from the control and dominance of evil forces.

If you are like I was before this revelation, you probably did not realize how valuable and significant time really was and still is. It wasn't until I received this revelation that I began to sense how valuable time is, how much I wasted, and how urgently, I needed to buy it (time) back for the Kingdom.

A great portion of my time was being used against me and much of the remaining portion was not being used to assist me. This was bondage and mental anguish for me. I desperately needed to be free. Thank God for the Spirit of Wisdom and revelation that changed my wrong perspective and misappropriation of "time." I wrote this poem to emphasize what time is to me now. I felt inspired to title it "If Time":

> If time were a mountain, it'd be Everest,
> If time were water, it'd be an Ocean,
> If time were a planet, it'd be Jupiter,
> If time were a resource, it'd be time!

Clearly, from this perspective, time is to be viewed as one of the three most important, invaluable and precious resources, or privileges God has given man.

Here is a thought that may help you remember the importance of managing your time. "Time will harvest for you whatever you sow it into, or spend it on. Truth is, if you continue to spend it on nothing, you will purchase and have nothing to show for it, regardless of how long you live".

How you chose to spend your time is paramount in determining the quality of life you will live. This is why you must recognize the importance of assigning your time specifically to accomplish your God given priorities. Which are assignments that have the ability to yield gratification in spite of obstacles?

"TIME NEEDS AN ASSIGNMENT"

To "assign," means to set apart or mark for a specific purpose. Designate as in an appointment; to appoint specifically, or to allot for something intentionally.

In this case your time should not be assigned by guessing, or assuming, but, by your understanding what the will of the Lord is for you specifically or what your priorities are presently.

This understanding will enable you to rescue as much time as you can from the evil forces and vices of this world. In other words, the Holy Spirit will empower through your yielding to His leadership a strategy to radically redeem or buy back your time from evil practices and worldly vices that you have fallen in bondage to habitually.

This freedom will allow you to see that no-one and no-thing can hold you in bondage, like you do yourself by choices and decisions for spending the most powerful and accessible resources you have, Time!

THE COST OF MISTAKEN PERCEPTION

In Matthew's Gospel, chapters 24 and 25, the use and mistaken perception of the value and importance of time is frequently stated as one of the primary reasons that God uses to determine the promotions or demotions of His stewards.

Renowned author Steven Covey, in his book "The Seven Habits of Highly Effective People" points out that "we gain control of time and events by seeing how they relate to our mission. The demands on our time are important or unimportant, urgent or not urgent. Important things serve our mission; unimportant things don't."

When we fail to establish aims or set goals that are related to our personal mission, many times things (unimportant) will seem to be more important that they are. A good example is an untimely or unanticipated phone call. You must develop the ability to not feel pressured to answer calls just because it's your telephone ringing, especially, when it interferes with an important task or project.

"TIME NEEDS ASSIGNMENT IN BUSINESS"

Richard Melton, a highly successful, accomplished and well-known businessman eventually learned that effective time management is one of the cornerstones of successful business management. He now explains, "You cannot expect to take control of your life and your business unless you are also firmly in control of your time."

Mr. Melton also asserts that, "Time Management is not something that you should apply only to your work. You should be applying it to all aspects of your life, to achieving your leisure and family and educational goals as well as your business or career goals. Because time is life, the purpose of time management is to turn you into a more effective user of that all-important resource."

Now, I must admit that I do not know Mr. Melton personally, nor have I ever been in his presence. However, I am familiar with many of his well-documented experiences and quotes. Even though, I cannot affirm his beliefs about Christ, one way or another. I can say this; Mr. Melton has certainly stated clearly a truth expressed throughout the pages of "Holy Writ", that **"Time is life"**. How we use it certainly determines the quality of life we will experience.

On another note, you must remember that because this most precious resource (time) must be managed by careful analysis, planning, and execution. Whenever you fail to assign your use of it specifically, your deeply rooted problem patterns of time management which may result from, indecision, inability to say no, lack of self-discipline, lack of planning, confusion in priorities, or lack of goals and objectives may resurface to create obstacles to your success.

Even sometimes success without the right application can create the illusion of ease, which may again result in ineffective and non-progressive living. Successful time management or effective management of you as a resource will require intentional focus, strong commitment, and hard work to turn it into an asset of favor.

"Time is an earthly trust that attracts many robbers" and it is TIME for you to realize this if you are going to maximize your purpose.

A method I now use to manage my time effectively was inspired during my devotion. I refer to it as "Time Zones".

"TIME ZONES"

The Holy Spirit helped me to simplify my daily approach to living by showing me how to separate my time into "Zones" to rank them by importance. Each of these zones is a period allotted for specific assignments to be accomplished.

First and most important is the **"Sacred Zone."** The Second period is the **"Business Zone."** The third period is [R-and-R] **"Rest and Recovery Zone."** The fourth period is the (REL) or "Recreation, Entertainment, and Leisure Zone." The fifth and final period I use a day or a series of 2-3 days of the last week of each month as a **"time of reflection."**

The first four foundational periods enable me to be effective from day to day by keeping me focused on my goals and objectives to be accomplished as I assign them.

The fifth period "Reflection" keeps me realistic about my goals/ expectations vs. my real accomplishments. During this time I'm usually able to do an **integrity check,** to see if I'm keeping my word or just making promises that sell me short as a liar. This may sound very strong but it's important that as children of God we practice keeping our word because after all we serve a God who *"Hastens to perform his word."*

It is amazing how much time I lose daily by wasting time with distractions and non-essential things without this structured arrangement.

The Sacred and Business Zones together account for the highest of *my time allotted priorities* because they determine the strength and continuity of my spiritual, mental, relational, and economical existence. How well I manage these zones speak directly to the productivity of my Faith, Family, and Business Focus.

Usually, if I fail to stay within the allotted parameters for either of these I get frustrated and loose my focus which greatly impacts my ability to be affective or productive. My "R-and-R" zone is designed for rest and recovery to keep me from burn-out. Often a lack of rest could affect my ability to be effective in many ways. The most difficult zone for me to manage has been my "REL" zone. So I've learned to make this zone a privilege I have to earn by making sure my checks and balances are in place.

Usually either of these three [recreation, entertainment, or relaxation] improperly managed could cost me quality time away from the zones that qualify me for the *"Good life that God prearranged for us to enjoy."* It's important to remember that God loves and rewards *"Diligence"* and promises that *"the hand of the diligent shall bear rule."*

I pray that you will continue to read so that the urgency of these "ingredients to structure" might assist you in your commitment to flourish in the Kingdom of God.

CHAPTER
10

Next I Must Understand Relationships

Are your Relationships helping you fly or fail?
You're most frequent associations
Impact your entire Life!

My Relationships Need Defining

"Keep **vigilant watch over your heart; that's where life starts.**
Don't talk out of both sides of your mouth; **avoid careless banter**, white
lies, and gossip. Keep your eyes straight ahead; **ignore all sideshow
distractions.** Watch your step, and the road will stretch out smooth
before you. Look neither right nor left; leave evil in the dust.

The dynamics of relationships are very interesting considering
the fact that all of us are born into primary relationships that have the
potential to shape and become a vibrant part of our lives through-out
our lifetime. As we grow-up, places we frequently visit and events or

functions we become a part of become **intersection points** for what may turn out to be a lasting friendship, business partnership or nightmare relationship that ends with lifetime scars.

When I was growing up I heard a teacher say in Elementary school that relationships are just like mathematics; they will add to you, subtract from you, multiply or divide you. My most consistent observation is that all relationships are a form of chemistry. Like chemicals the balance or volatility of each is determined by mixtures of personality, need, maturity or development, core values, goals, self discipline, purpose and timing.

Understanding how to discern and define through the wisdom of God the type of relationships you are in and their significant goal or purpose is essential for effective lifestyle management.

We are all dysfunctional in that we were "born in sin and shaped in iniquity" which means that all of our ways may seem right to us while having negative impact on those connected to us. As children of God we must learn how to turn all of our relational dysfunctions and liabilities into assets.

A few years ago the Holy Spirit taught me how to use "4 Ps" to make this happen: problems, principles, processes, and privileges. Whenever there is a **problem** we must seek out the Kingdom **principle**, engage the **process** according to it, and experience the **privilege**. This is the joy of having access to Kingdom righteousness. Through this method we move from problems to privileges in our relationships to preserve our unity and peace.

"Love Trouble"

Two men sat in the lobby early on a Monday morning waiting to see me for counsel. One was holding his head as if he could explode any moment, while the other starred straight up towards the ceiling as if he could penetrate it by the intensity of his laser stair. As the receptionist entered the lobby to escort the first candidate to his appointment, the exit door burst open with a loud noise, slamming into the wall and in came a newly wedded mother nearly dragging her two-year-old son, screaming and cursing at her husband who was shouting "I'm tired of your__ foolishness and I've had all I'm going to take from you."

All too frequently we discover that **relationships can be easy to enter into but in many cases difficult to manage.** Whether it's your heartthrob, best friend, business partner, parents, mentor, siblings or simply an infrequent associate all relationships require skills; Re-lat-ion-ship skills. I'm talking about disciplines that must first be discovered, then practiced until they forge for us the principle power to guide our hearts in spite of how we feel about issues we confront every single day of our lives in relationships.

Easier to fall in Love than Stay in Love

Are you aware that approximately one out of every two marriages in the United States ends in divorce? This statistic was not such a problem during the seventies when I first started in ministry because they reflected the secular society more than the church. But today the numbers reflect both the secular and the church.

Another alarming stat is that, "out of the couples that do remain married, a good number are no longer in love, or happy together, despite the fact that they aren't divorced." Also single parent families and blended families are leading issues that demand God's urgent wisdom in today's society.

Clearly, It's easy to get into relationships but difficult to manage them

Everyone wants strong, loving and healthy relationships. No one plans to fail or fall out of love in a relationship. But it happens. And when it happens it hurts.

In the beginning there's always that **"magical chemistry"** that causes us to see one another as special, exciting and necessary. But as time transpires and he or she no longer agrees with all your ideas and begin expressing displeasures about your behaviors, the indifference and conflict starts eating away that intense feeling of love and fondness.

Suddenly, you awake one morning and begin to notice that the tolerance you once displayed towards the persons faults and irritating behaviors is no longer there. What happened to the magic? Or where did the love go? How did the excitement and attraction turn into boredom and disinterest? Why did trust and respect turn into hurt and resentment? Whose responsibility was it to keep the love strong and vibrant?

As a counselor, I know that behavioral psychologists say that "all of these questions really ask the same thing, *why we fall out of love?*" Usually our first response is "It's the other persons fault." But there are many things that can be factored in as you grow and mature in relationships.

THREE PRIMARY PRINCIPLES

There are three **primary laws** or principles that we all need to be aware of in order to "diligently guard our hearts," and proactively manage how we function in relationships. They are love, wisdom, and honor.

In the Kingdom of God system there is an interchangeable overlapping quality associated with all life and relationship governing principles. Faith which is the function of God is to be seen as the **covering** for all our exchanges in righteousness. Everything we do should be done by, in, or through "Faith." When we fail to exchange by faith, all of our conversations, judgments, confrontations, adversities and favors, are responses from our lower nature, *"Whatever is not of Faith is SIN."*

For instance, in the Kingdom system, faith is the activator and love is the motivator. Faith activates Kingdom love and love motivates godly faith empowered by the Holy Spirit to promote righteous exchanges that glorify God.

Law 1: Love is most essential because it empowers us to live a self-less life that places no unnecessary demands on others in relationship to us. It is a godly love which ensures that we have right *motives* ourselves first. Especially, in that we are required to "Love our neighbors as our self."

This makes us better able to embrace others genuinely, and be better equipped to serve their concerns without including our own selfish expectations or demands. Here the nine "fruit of the spirit" must be practiced and nurtured from within us in all of our exchanges. Whenever we fail to be guided by them we fall short of interacting in the way that pleases or glorifies God.

This is the "Perfect love which cast out all fears, or the Charity that never fails, which allows others to know that we are Christ disciples because we love and serve one another by it. On this impactful display of Kingdom righteousness "hang all the prophets and the law."

Law 2: Wisdom is the second law because it assumes both the government and regulation of successful love from a Christ-centered perspective. In other words Wisdom directs and measures out the **timing, type,** and **allotment portions** of love to be shared, to keep us from unrealistic demands or expectations from those we interact with. "Wisdom is the principle thing" because it teaches proper or appropriate ethics for every exchange.

In other words, some relationships **require more service**, while others **require more conversation**. Yet others **may require both**. Some **hierarchal relationships** may even demand more loyalty and openness because of the indeterminate warfare that evolves from positions of power and influence.

Here is also where we use principle wisdom to employ and distinguish between **Physical** love (eros), **Family** love (storge), **Affectionate** love (philia), or **Divine** love (agape) which is *the love that God commands* even if someone does not appeal to us, we can still treat them right and do all we can to help build them up in the faith.

Here wisdom also enables us to understand how to properly

exchange what we know as the correct distinction of "Love's" fruit, so we are always able to guard and protect our heart from wrong perceptions.

Depending on who you are and what God has planned for your future, wrong perceptions driven by personal offenses may ultimately force you to draft wrong conclusions that make you vulnerable to wrong company and conversations which will result in a forfeit of God's best in your life.

Law 3: Honor ensures that we give to and extract from proper positional graces, human agencies, ordained connections and associations the provisions and respect that God requires.

But honor first recognizes the need to discriminate (demonstrate extra caution/special reverence) where "authority" is present or "orders" are given. Your decision to "honor" the natural and spiritual chain of authority is the bridge to covenant natural and spiritual blessings. **This is why we say that honor is the seed for "Access."**

Hebrews chapters 12 and 13 says: "And you have forgotten the exhortation which speaks to you as to sons:

"My son, do not despise the chastening of the LORD, Nor be discouraged when you are rebuked by Him; for whom the LORD loves He chastens, and scourges every son whom He receives."

If you endure chastening, God deals with you as with sons; for what son is there whom a father does not chasten? But if you are without chastening, of which all have become partakers, then you are illegitimate and not sons. Furthermore, we have had human fathers who corrected us, and we paid them respect.

Shall we not much more readily be in subjection to the Father of spirits and live? For they indeed for a few days chastened us as **seemed** *best to them,* **but He for our profit,** *that we may be partakers of His holiness. Now no chastening seems to be joyful for the present, but painful; nevertheless, afterward it yields the peaceable fruit of righteousness to those who have been trained by it."*

Problem is that many Kingdom citizens do not experience *the peaceable fruit of righteousness* because they cannot endure indifference long enough to be trained by it. Here we must be willing to endure hardness as good soldiers understanding that the Kingdom is always under assault, but the violent take it by force.

I can recall many times when I would attempt to prove that I could justify my offenses, the Holy Spirit would say to me that **"offense is the test of spiritual maturity."** It is the distinguishing mark of the *character of God on display* when we respond to offenses totally from faith. It is the primary reason why the body of Christ is divided and therefore demands that all Kingdom citizens handle both favorable and unfavorable relational exchanges strictly according to the word of God.

PROBLEM WITH PERCEPTIONS

If you fall in love enough times with people who "change" on you, your mind might actually move to the next stage of rationalization: **that something is wrong with you!** After all you pick the wrong people over and over again. Your disappointment and frustration may turn into anger and apathy: If you falsely evaluate your experiences you may find yourself saying, "Relationships are not for me because they cause too much pain. I'd rather just not get involved. That way I want get hurt."

You might conclude that love and relationships is too difficult to manage, and resolve to live peacefully alone. Or—and this may be the saddest choice of all; you might decide to stay in a relationship that is purely a liability because it's a risk to your existence. Neither of these examples is acceptable if you are going to fulfill your life's purpose.

Most relationship counselors will tell you that it's natural for any relationship to become "comfortable," and it's unrealistic to expect to feel intensely in love with a partner all the time, after being together a long time. Some experts even advise today's married couples to "Accept the lost of romance in marriage, and become companions." But this conventional advice does not agree with the Wisdom of God.

Notice 1 Corinthians 7:1-7, *"Now, getting down to the questions you asked in your letter to me. First, is it a good thing to have sexual relations? Certainly—but only within a certain context. It's good for a man to have a wife, and for a woman to have a husband.*

Sexual drives are strong, but marriage is strong enough to contain them and provide for a balanced and fulfilling sexual life in a world of sexual disorder. **The marriage bed must be a place of mutuality—** *the husband seeking to satisfy his wife, the wife seeking to satisfy her husband.*

Marriage is not a place to "stand up for your rights." Marriage is a decision to serve the other, whether in bed or out. *Abstaining from sex is permissible for a period of time if you both agree to it, and if it's for the purposes of prayer and fasting—but only for such times.*

Then come back together again. **Satan has an ingenious way of** *tempting us when we least expect it. I'm not, understand, commanding these periods of abstinence—only providing my best counsel if you should choose them."*

Let me encourage you that just because so many fail at love and marriage does not mean that love is meant to fail! I believe without an ounce of doubt that it is possible to keep love strong and nurture strong relationships of every kind. *"With God all things are possible!"*

KEEPING THE LEVERAGE OF LOVE IS POSSIBLE

You must commit to mastering the art of love and relationships by learning the rules and principles that govern their success. Every kind of relationship is subject to the "laws and Principles" that govern it. This is the first and the most important part of the process that makes us "fit for relationships." Keep in mind that it will still require hard work. The first year of our marriage I heard someone say that

The First Principle: Making Love and Relationships Last!

Since that time and after thirty years of serving as a pastor, pre-marital counselor, addiction-, spousal-, and drug-abuse counselor, parent-child/mentoring counselor and of course being a part of an exciting marriage just a few months shy of thirty years, with four adult children, two sons-in-law and five beautiful grandchildren, the statement is certainly accurate.

The vast majority of singles and couples that have come in for counsel have absolutely no clue that principles and laws are in place to ensure their success in relationships. Both, I and my wife, Denise agree that learning the right perspectives and disciplines of love and applying them are the first secrets to succeeding in "relationships."

Still today there are multitudes of persons who are not aware of this Secret!

I once heard someone say, "If you never learn how to use love constructively, then love ends up using you." But it also true that anything you don't know how to use instructively [including love] to create the results you want, will leave you making the same mistakes over and over again.

This is why I say definitively that your love and relationships need "**Wisdom.**" *Wisdom is the principle thing, therefore get Wisdom, but in all of your getting get understanding."* Principle wisdom in relationships helps you invest appropriately, the successful portions and discern accurately the different kinds of allotments of love to extend so that your heart is not made more vulnerable than it has to be. Like I mentioned in my "time allotments" you must have sacred relationships, business relationships, R-and-R relationships (those who assist and allow you to rest and recover), and also it is good practice to have REL or "recreation, entertainment, and leisure associates." And finally, I use a day or a series of two or three days of the last week of each month as a time of reflection with a combination of my family, peers, and directors who are personally impacted by my decisions.

Again notice the caution Solomon advises before warning to diligently guard the heart, *"When I was a boy at my father's knee, the pride and joy of my mother, He would sit me down and drill me: "Take this to heart. Do what I tell you—live!*

Sell everything and buy wisdom! Forage for Understanding! Don't forget one word! Don't deviate an inch! Never walk away from Wisdom— she guards your life; love her—she keeps her eye on you. Above all and before all, do this: Get Wisdom! Write this at the top of your list:

Get understanding! Throw your arms around her—believe me, you won't regret it; never let her go—she'll make your life glorious. She'll garland your life with grace, she'll festoon your days with beauty." Dear friend, take my advice; it will add years to your life. I'm writing out clear directions to wisdom way, I'm drawing a map to righteous road. I don't want you ending up in blind alleys, or wasting time making wrong turns.

*Hold tight to good advice; don't relax your grip. **Guard it well— your life is at stake!** Don't take Wicked Bypass; don't so much as set foot on that road. Stay clear of it; give it a wide berth.*

*Make a detour and be on your way. **Evil people are restless unless they're making trouble; they can't get a good night's sleep unless they've made life miserable for somebody.** Perversity is their food and drink, violence their drug of choice.*

***The ways of right-living people glow with light;** the longer they live, the brighter they shine. But the road of wrongdoing gets darker and darker—travelers can't see a thing; they fall flat on their faces.*

The Importance of the Nine Fruits of the Spirit

But the fruit of the [Holy] Spirit [the work which His presence within accomplishes] is love, joy (gladness), peace, patience (an even temper, forbearance), kindness, goodness (benevolence), faithfulness, Gentleness (meekness, humility), self-control (self-restraint, continence). Against such things there is no law [that can bring a charge]. And those who belong to Christ Jesus (the Messiah) have crucified the flesh (the godless human nature) with its passions and appetites and desires. (Galatians 5:22-26, AMP)

If we live by the [Holy] Spirit, let us also walk by the Spirit. *[If by the Holy Spirit we have our life in God, let us go forward walking in line, our conduct controlled by the Spirit.] Let us not become vainglorious and self-conceited, competitive and challenging and provoking and irritating to one another, envying and being jealous of one another.*

These nine fruits are designed to establish the parameters for all of our relational exchanges both with God and our fellowman. You can master relationships the same way you learn to master a cell phone, or develop any skill by allowing the instructions to determine your usage. But until you are aware of what you have been doing, you have no choice but to continue doing it.

Notice how the fruit of the human spirit that are planted in us by the Holy Spirit are designed to assist us against dysfunctional behavior.

But what happens when we live God's way? He brings gifts into our lives, much the same way that fruit appears in an orchard—things like affection for others, exuberance about life, serenity. We develop a willingness to stick with things, a sense of compassion in the heart, and a conviction that a basic holiness permeates things and people.

We find ourselves involved in loyal commitments, not needing to force our way in life, able to marshal and direct our energies wisely.

Legalism is helpless in bringing this about; it only gets in the way. Among those who belong to Christ, everything connected with getting our own way and mindlessly responding to what everyone else calls necessities is killed off for good—crucified.

Since this is the kind of life we have chosen, the life of the Spirit, let us make sure that we do not just hold it as an idea in our heads or a sentiment in our hearts, but work out its implications in every detail of our lives. That means we will not compare ourselves with each other as if one of us were better and another worse. We have far more interesting things to do with our lives. Each of us are an original (the Message).

Here, the emphasis must be clear that "if" we decide to walk in the Spirit we will not fulfill the lust of our flesh. I suggest you continue to journey along with me through the laws and principles designed to govern the success of all relationships so that you can gain total victory as you learn and apply those you need. Remember *"Whatever is born of God overcomes the world through faith"*.

Measuring Your Relationships

A good way to measure if you are in truly healthy relationships is by using the Three Es; along with scriptural guidance. The three E's are *Excitement, Esteem, and Ease.*

I use them to help me determine whether I'm comfortable with the type of exchanges or communication that takes place during frequent, random, or scheduled events or occasions.

If one of these three E's is difficult to experience then I try to make adjustments consciously using familiar Principles that will prepare me to respond more favorably the next time. I often do this to create a winning fellowship for the two of us or the group, depending upon the relationship's importance or correspondence, which I'll discuss more as I go forward.

Excitement and *optimism for the future*... If I'm happy relationally and/or in love, right connections encourage me to look forward to tomorrow with excitement. Nothing generates future optimism like right relationships.

*I only over-rule this emotion where honoring or submitting to Authority is required. Be careful to always yield in this case and God will fulfill His promise in your life. See Acts 9 and 10; 1 Samuel 16.

Esteem and *self-confidence*... A good relationship regardless of its type will support you in feeling high self-esteem at all times and will do nothing to tarnish it.

Ease in *being your-self*... In all supportive relationships, you will find it *easy to be yourself* around your partners, your friends, and in all circumstances. If for some reason you keep having to change "who you are" to please them or to fit in the fellowship, it's time for re-evaluation to determine **the type of association** you have categorically with the person or group.

The three E's will develop over time in all truly healthy and growing relationships. But true love thrives only under certain conditions. This is where I recommend that you take charge. In order to stay in love, *you must consciously create those conditions necessary for love to grow.* Then you will naturally behave in all the ways the laws and principles tell you to behave in order to stay in love.

Use 1 Corinthians 13 to solidify yourself in making proper adjustments with right motives in your love walk because true loves test *your "motives"* more than it does **others**.

The Way of Love: Primary laws of relationships

If I speak with human eloquence and angelic ecstasy but don't love, I'm nothing but the creaking of a rusty gate. If I speak God's Word with power, revealing all his mysteries and making everything plain as day, and if I have faith that says to a mountain, "Jump," and it jumps, but I don't love, I'm nothing. If I give everything I own to the poor and even go to the stake to be burned as a martyr, but I don't love, I've gotten nowhere.

So, no matter what I say, what I believe, and what I do, I'm bankrupt without love. Love never gives up. Love cares more for others than for self. Love doesn't want what it doesn't have. Love doesn't strut, Doesn't have a swelled head, Doesn't force itself on others, Isn't always "me first," Doesn't fly off the handle, Doesn't keep score of the sins of others, Doesn't revel when others grovel, Takes pleasure in the flowering of truth, Puts up with anything, Trusts God always, Always looks for the best, Never looks back, But keeps going to the end.

Love never dies. *Inspired speech will be over some day; praying in tongues will end; understanding will reach its limit. We know only a portion of the truth, and what we say about God is always incomplete. But when the Complete arrives, our incompletes will be canceled.*

When I was an infant at my mother's breast, I gurgled and cooed like any infant. When I grew up, I left those infant ways for good. We don't yet see things clearly. We're squinting in a fog, peering through a mist. But it won't be long before the weather clears and the sun shines bright! We'll see it all then, see it all as clearly as God sees us, knowing him directly just as he knows us!

But for right now, until that completeness, we have three things to do to lead us toward that consummation: Trust steadily in God, hope unswervingly, love extravagantly. **And the best of the three is love.** (1 Corinthians 13, The Message)

A very insightful teacher I learned a great deal from in the early eighties, while watching her late night programs, Dr. Barbara De Angelis said, "One thing that we do to ourselves as humans is fool ourselves and others when it comes to knowing what we are feeling. But the one area you cannot control easily is your body. If you insist to me that you are not upset about something, and I hook you up to an instrument that measures physiological responses, your body would not lie. It would tell me that you were upset, even if you denied it."

Emotional excitement is a natural reaction to certain conditions. When those conditions are absent or inhibited, so is your natural emotional response. The thing that is most fortunate about this is that your emotions guided by the Holy Spirit are great barometers to telling you how well your relationship is working, and when it/they need more attention.

The scripture identify three behavioral qualities that must be developed in each of us to be effective in our relationships and maintain enjoyment. They are; the ability to be **open**, the ability to be **honest**, and the ability to **confront others effectively**.

When used properly these three behaviors will help you to generate and preserve strong relationships that will assist you in experiencing a joyful and peaceful life. Read the NIV version of Galatians chapters one and two.

Notice the proactive scripture measures Paul used to protect and preserve brotherhood fellowship using all three measures.

Paul Accepted by the Apostles

Fourteen years later, I went up again to Jerusalem, this time with Barnabas. I took Titus along also. I went in response to a revelation and set before them the gospel that I preach among the Gentiles. But I did this privately to those who seemed to be leaders; for fear that I was running or had run my race in vain. Open.

Yet not even Titus, who was with me, was compelled to be circumcised, even though he was a Greek. This matter arose because some false brothers had infiltrated our ranks to spy on the freedom we have in Christ Jesus and to make us slaves. We did not give in to them for a moment, so that the truth of the gospel might remain with you.

As for those who seemed to be important—whatever they were makes no difference to me; God does not judge by external appearance—

those men added nothing to my message. On the contrary, they saw that I had been entrusted with the task of preaching the gospel to the Gentiles, just as Peter had been to the Jews.

For God, who was at work in the ministry of Peter as an apostle to the Jews, was also at work in my ministry as an apostle to the Gentiles. James, Peter and John, those reputed to be pillars, gave me and Barnabas the right hand of fellowship when they recognized the grace given to me. They agreed that we should go to the Gentiles, and they to the Jews. All they asked was that we should continue to remember the poor, the very thing I was eager to do. **HONEST**

Paul Opposes Peter

When Peter came to Antioch, I opposed him to his face, because he was clearly in the wrong. Before certain men came from James, he used to eat with the Gentiles. But when they arrived, he began to draw back and separate himself from the Gentiles because he was afraid of those who belonged to the circumcision group. The other Jews joined him in his hypocrisy, so that by their hypocrisy even Barnabas was led astray.

When I saw that they were not acting in line with the truth of the gospel, I said to Peter in front of them all, *"You are a Jew, yet you live like a Gentile and not like a Jew. How is it, then, that you force Gentiles to follow Jewish customs?*

"We who are Jews by birth and not 'Gentile sinners' 16know that a man is not justified by observing the law, but by faith in Jesus Christ. So we, too, have put our faith in Christ Jesus that we may be justified by faith in Christ and not by observing the law, because by observing the

law no one will be justified.

"If, while we seek to be justified in Christ, it becomes evident that we ourselves are sinners does that mean that Christ promotes sin? **Absolutely not! If I rebuild what I destroyed, I prove that I am a lawbreaker.** For through the law I died to the law so that I might live for God.

I have been crucified with Christ and I no longer live, but Christ lives in me. The life I live in the body, I live by faith in the Son of God, who loved me and gave himself for me. 21I do not set aside the grace of God, for if righteousness could be gained through the law, Christ died for nothing!"

Effective Confrontation

An intense study of Kingdom relationships made me aware of the appropriate wisdom [the second law of relationships] of fellowshipping the "Anointed and Appointed Authority" of God.

A good question to ask yourself depending upon the type of relationship you're encountering is "am I a better performer, or am I more skillful in **frequent** associations, **random** associations, or **specially planned** associations; with this particular person or group of persons. This principle is called the **"Law or Principle of Associations."**

Sometimes you may or may not feel accepted, or you may actually be the one rejecting the other person or persons because of an offense, unspoken trespass, or an unsettled account. In either case along *with the Holy Spirit, your emotions* are trying to get you to be honest about what you feel, so you may seek the proper way to bring closure in your relational exchanges to allow you and others to maintain a sense of peace and spiritual rest regarding each other during fellowship.

Keep in mind that God does not bring us into each other's lives to fragment and separate us; that would make *"body unity"* or the unity of the faith an un-obtainable reality. *"Two are better than one"* simply means that we are suppose to make each other better.

Proverbs 17:17 says *"Friends love [at all times] through all kinds of weather, and families stick together in all kinds of trouble."* The commentary says of this passage, "No change of outward circumstances should abate our affection for our friends or relatives. But no friend, except Christ, deserves unlimited confidence.

In John 15:13 Jesus said *"I've told you these things for a purpose: that my joy might be your joy, and your joy wholly mature. This is my command:* Love one another the way I loved you. This is the very best way to love. Put your life on the line for your friends. *You are my friends when you do the things I command you. I'm no longer calling you servants because servants don't understand what their master is thinking and planning. No, I've named you friends because I've let you in on everything I've heard from the Father."*

Here the lesson is layered with several dimensions of truth that I've discussed in the book that is the sequel to this book titled **"Your Divine relationships need defining"** before your friendships and inappropriate associations distort your purpose.

Two things Jesus points out in the original language regarding this passage: First, A true pastor/shepherd *"puts his life on the line for those he elevates from "servants to friends"* and **Second,** *"He only let's them in on everything their Pastor/mentor is thinking and planning* *because they are considered his inner circle/Permanent friends"* in lifetime partnerships.

There is a great certainty that you will meet many more temporary friends and associates than *permanent*. So, do not allow your heart to become overly sentimental and attached, especially depending upon the type of position you hold in people's lives, because when temporary friendships are improperly defined as permanent, we do ourselves and our purpose a great injustice. By committing too much confidentiality to people who may turn as enemies and use our inside personal or sacred information that we only share out of trust while mutually bonded in a way that seemed to convey friendship forever.

Some positions are highly transitional due to the constant increase or decrease in population, participation, personal growth or maturity, organizational shifts or demands for changes, information and communication flow, leadership design, decision-making, and personnel chemistry. So you must always maintain your primary perspective from a positional point of view to stay effective and bring such leverage to those impacted by your post.

I'm not saying you will be perfect in this because we are human and our needs and wants sometimes shift from one day to the next. But as a rule of thumb, you must stay conscious of the fact that one decision or a single person added or deleted from the group may severely affect the dynamics of what once was a strong team or friendship.

This is a situation that happens much more frequent than it should, but until the revelation of divine relationships become frequent lessons in the body of Christ the dishonor and disregard for divine relationships will continue to manifest because many persons don't have time to learn the correct way to function in relationships.

This discovery I made after the Holy Spirit revealed to me that, **"My relationships need defining."** Here I was given a primary principle that was designed to assist me in guarding my heart diligently, especially in relationships.

Always remember that "Divine Relationships" are as divinely initiated as the relationship between Adam and Eve. This special relationship that was orchestrated by the finger of God was not exempt from Lucifer's influence which resulted in the fall.

When the fall of man in Gen. 3 is examined against; the transfer of the power of multiplication, the influence to subdue, and dominion over "all" creatures of the earth *[including the most subtle beast of the field]* in Genesis 1; 27-28, IMMEDIATELY we see that God expected man to operate in the earth according to instructional knowledge of laws and principles that were designed to govern the responsibility He gave them.

God Does Not Give Responsibility
Without His Ability to Perform or Carry it Out

You need to notice that God did not interfere with the *illegal communication* that transpired between Satan and Eve because He had already given specific orders to both Adam and Eve as created spiritual beings, "made in His image, after His likeness" about their one regulation and specific responsibility to Him as their chief oversight.

*Notice "God said, Let Us [Father, Son, and Holy Spirit] make mankind in Our image, after Our likeness, and **"let them" have complete authority** over the fish of the sea, the birds of the air, the [tame] **beasts,** and **over all of the earth,** and over **everything that creeps** upon the earth. So God created man in His own image, in the image and likeness of God He created him; male and female He created them. And **God blessed them and said to them,** Be fruitful, multiply, and fill the earth, and **subdue** it [using all its vast resources in the service of God and man]; **and have dominion over** the fish of the sea, the birds of the air, and over **every living creature that moves upon the earth."***

Before I go further, let's explore how we got ~to this point

Let's begin with a question, What is it that causes us to feel that we know how to preserve Love and develop successful relationships when the majority of us are probably not aware of who taught us how to do either? Isn't it interesting that we can account for many of our teachers regarding important areas of our lives, but fail to identify any single person as our love and relationship instructor's?

Even though no one probably sat you down and explained the "secrets of successful relationships", "The primary laws and principles of relationships", or taught you how to communicate your feelings properly. Yet, when you were growing up you spent countless hours learning how to have a relationship.

You may be trying to figure out where? How would you accept it if I told you right in your own home! In fact, you've been learning from the time you were born up until now. You have actually been an apprentice to your parents and all the older members of your family. This is inevitable.

You learned how to laugh, cry, shut down, yell out, deceive one another, manipulate the facts to get your way, and hide your feelings. You've learned how to imitate your parents or guardians much better than you realize. The message to a child is clear "corrupt communication destroys good manners" or "Train consistently, with intense diligence the child while he is young and eventually he will conceive the importance of good behavior." Because "children left to rear themselves will usually bring their parents to shame."

Are you aware that most people when asked *"do you want your relationship to duplicate your parents"* answer with emphatic energy, *"No"*? So my question is what are you doing to make sure your relationships doesn't turn out that way?

Some of you are friends or family with people who are terrible at relationships. But, you listen to their advice about what you should do. There is an old saying, *"To determine the future of your relationships; take a good look at your advisers!"*

You must realize that people who complain about their parents or other relationships they never want to turn out like, usually duplicate them if they fail to get new information and make plans to do differently.

In my book on relationships I list several biblical and modern examples of people who, despite themselves, grew up to relate to others just as their parents related to each other:

While your parents unconsciously taught you certain attitudes about relationships; society taught you another set of messages using a variety of sources.

We Live in a Diverse and Transitional World Relationally

The dynamics and infrastructure of our relationships are always evolving from one age to the next, one culture to the next, and one generation to the next. Has it ever occurred to you that according to the Bible, man's earthly problem only began after he was put into relationship with his own kind "woman"?

Eve must have been a lot of "Man," "Woo,-Man!" Through *disorderly, inappropriate communication* she became the instrument that Satan used to influence the spiritual death of a man who only had fellowship with God prior to this occasion.

As long as Adam was able to function within his assignment without the distraction of having to communicate with another "human" like himself, or someone designed to assist him he appeared to be doing well.

But as soon as God put him to sleep and fashioned a "Helpmate", *suitable for him* to fulfill his God-given purpose, Satan became interested in his *help* more than him [Adam]. This is a very prominent piece of understanding that I pray you will grasp, especially if you are going to succeed in your God given assignments.

It is also very important that you learn to value important connections so that you learn how to discriminate your relationships by importance and correspondence. This must be done in the same like manner as you manage to discriminate your relationships with your natural parents and siblings. There are both Natural and Spiritual Laws and Principles in place to assist you in knowing how to maintain your correct posture in times of indifference and pressure.

In all divinely appointed relationships [starting with Eve's appointment to Adam] Satan is attracted immediately because he understands the importance of *timing and maturity* for the accomplishment of *identity and purpose*. This is one of the primary reasons why Jesus pointed out that *"The kingdom is always under assault"*. I'll discuss "Divine connections" and "Satanic attractions" more as we progress, but first let's look at the historical evolution of relationships to determine why your "relationships must be defined."

The significant impact of the
Historical Evolution of Relationships

Not far removed from the entrance of Satan into human nature, Genesis 4 allows us a glimpse into the progression of "SIN" [Satan In Nature] to witness an elder brother commit "fratricide" against his younger brother. In this account we immediately see what it means to be *"conceived in sin, and shaped in iniquity"* which also exposes our human frailties and high levels of social dysfunctions.

Just two generations into the society as we now know it and already we were confronted with an urgent need to search out the laws and principles that govern the functionality of successful relationships.

As I begin with the past and bring it up to this present age. Notice how the dynamics of relationships and their purpose have changed over the last sixty years. Traditionalists were born before 1946, they are known as Veterans. Baby Boomers were born between 1946 and 1964. Generation X was born between 1965-1976, known as Computer Age and Internet Generation. And the Millennial: Born between 1977 and 2000, also known as Generation "Y," Internet and Digital Age.

To put relationships in historical perspective growing up in the fifties and sixties, the period known as the "Traditionalist" was extremely different than today. Also during the sixties and seventies the "Baby Boomers" were presented with different relationship challenges than the Traditionalist as they begin realizing how swiftly the structure and purpose of relationships were changing because of computer technology and advance communication.

A senior I interviewed commented that "our relationships changed tremendously during that time in many good and bad ways."

Too further gain some historical perspective on the evolution of relationships. How would it affect you to know that "Your great-great-great-grand parents more than likely married during the time when *"marriage was more of a business arrangement than a romantic endeavor?"* A woman married so she could have someone to take care of her, but a man married to have someone to bear his children and provide a home for them. Happiness and love [the first law of relationships] were bonuses.

Often, the task of physical and financial survival took so much time and effort that staying in love, having a good sex life, and developing one's sense of self were all trivial matters compared with making enough money and hoping the land would yield enough crops to get through the winter.

Our great grand parents' generation had it a little easier in most cases. But marriage and having children were still considered the only acceptable choices. Only in the past forty to fifty years have men and women been free to choose whether or not they wanted to have a relationship and/or marry.

Widespread use of contraception, changing morality, the emerging role of women as equals in work and in relationships; all these factors influenced the transformation of relationships from an economic necessity and a social and religious obligation to one of personal choice.

Since the 1970s, we in this society have entered into relationships not out of necessity or duty, but out of choice. That means that your expectations about what you get back from your relationship are much higher than your parents' expectations were. Today you seek intangible things from relationships. Things like intimacy, mutual belief systems, balance of power, and support in pursuing your individual sense of self.

Our ancestors were prepared and trained for their roles in marriage: Women were taught how to care for the children and make a home; men were taught how to make a living. But no one was trained how to create intimacy, how to balance the power between yourself and your partner, or how to communicate openly about sex.

Although, we now have the freedom to do what we want with our relationships, we don't always have the knowledge we need to do it successfully. So, it all comes down to you. You have the freedom to learn how to have successful relationships, it's your responsibility. Today you can't blame your parents, friends, partners, or society for teaching you. Through Godly "wisdom" empowered by the Holy Spirit you have the power to do something about your life.

A great part of effective living is correspondence based upon a clear and definitive understanding of oneself. When we know who we are, what we are here for, and where we are going in life, then we are better prepared thru specific understanding to determine who's going or the type of persons we must select to go with us.

When we discover the truth about relationships in scripture it becomes increasingly clear that persons who are considered *Destiny travelers or Divine connections* are more of a bridge than a burden, asset than liability. They also add to us and multiply us, more than subtracts from and divide us.

You must understand that with all humans there is a level of dysfunction, but the distinct privilege of destiny companions is that the two key principles of co-habitation are constantly manifested, which are grounded in the *Law of Love; first, to know who you are in Christ. And second, to be liberated to fulfill your purpose daily* as a son of God, because of a proper perspective of the empowerment of divine Love.

This statement, "Your relationships need defining" continued to resonate in my spirit, until I began seeing visions and dreams of how relationships properly fitted and wisely or skillfully connected, empower and generate constant flow and efficient progress to peaceful, dynamic co-habitations, fulfillment of purpose, and the acceptance and appreciation of one's self.

One of the immediate discoveries that surfaced from this observation deals with how improper connections whether, pipes, fittings, faucets, pumps or valves; or simply generators, wires, transformers, transmitters and sockets design to supply water or electricity, are intended to service, they may eventually erupt and cause lasting harm with impending doom.

Just as these connections require skillful planning, prudent selections, purposeful coordination and right fittings; our lives must be similarly ordered so we may experience daily fulfillment and purposeful living. After all, that is what Jesus came to give us, *"Life (God's kind) and that more abundantly,"* (John 10:10).

The Apostle Paul points out in Ephesians 2:10 that, *"We are God's handiwork, recreated in Christ Jesus, that we may do those good works which God predestined or planned beforehand for us, that we should walk in them living the good life which He prearranged and made ready for us to live."*

This prearranged good life actually confirms the need for the wisdom of Proverbs 4:26, *"ponder and consider well the path of your feet, and let all your ways be established and ordered aright."* (AMP)

Too often we violate our essence and spend our lives in misery because of improper relationship connections that are made prematurely. The simple truth is, everybody can't go with you if you are going to fulfill your "Life's purpose." Your life purpose is what I describe as destiny.

Even though, in this life *there are many good people* who can travel with you from one city to another, you must realize that destiny travelers are more for the fulfillment of your life's purpose than pleasures.

Since the purpose you are here is a "Divine purpose" that you are called to fulfill, your relationships should be viewed as "Divine Relationships." The Kingdom of God gives us the privilege of experiencing God through three Divine Connections which are put in place for your growth and development both in relations to Him as your Father and to your assignment among men.

These *three relationships* are The Word, The Holy Spirit, and Your Spiritual Guide or Shepherd. Each of these connections honored properly will prepare you in Righteousness or Right standing with God and man. This is the cure for dysfunctional Social Behavior that became a part of our lives through ignorance.

In both natural and spiritual life we grow through three phases or stages that complete the reciprocal cycle of our social development. We are first Dependent [at birth/needy], Independent [through mentoring/ responsible], and Inter-dependant [to reciprocate and give-back] to those who assumed responsibility for our dependency.

Here you must understand that the same law of "Honor" required of children regarding their natural parents is the same spiritual law that is robbing the body of Christ of its inheritance spiritually. The third principle of the Kingdom that is assigned to govern and regulate relationships is the "Law of Honor."

Honor is not agreement; it is to hold in high esteem, to mark as different, to respect on another level. As I stated earlier it also means payment, because God made it obligatory for "long life and that it might be well with you."

Don't you think something is wrong when you are more comfortable with sustaining systems that had no responsible hand in your development and the giving of honor not earned to someone you barely know. Are you are able to justify this folly because of an offense, disagreement or hidden dislike for those who labored to develop you during your dependant years?

Even though this happens frequently naturally and spiritually with our siblings it is dysfunctional behavior that God will not bless. God's blessing comes through submission to authority and a commitment to honor authority for the sake of transferring Godly inheritance.

This is why He is referred to as the God of Abraham, Isaac, and Jacob.

Divine Relationships are branch/vine connections

Though we have ten thousand instructors "We have not many fathers".

This means that everyone will not be able to fit within your life's demands because: First, Your Destiny is frequently assaulted by spiritual warfare and adversaries that thrive *on wrong relationships*, procrastinations, bad choices, *improper assignments* or connections that *distort purpose*.

Second, Many destiny travelers become a part of our lives by appointment; so you must be *trained to discern* and *effectively adapt* to them because they are assigned for *specific purposes* at *critical stages* in our development which bridges us over to our next mark or phase in destiny. I call these "leveraging graces" (Acts 9:1-19, 10:1-48).

There are two type of "Leveraging Graces", permanent [stabilizers or fixed pillars] and temporary [momentary deposits for *seasons* or *reasons*]. Here, life in relationship should be seen as a house in construction that requires both permanent supports and temporarily installed pillars to hold up weight until the adjustments can be made.

Saul's Conversion

Meanwhile, Saul was still breathing out murderous threats against the Lord's disciples. He went to the high priest and asked him for letters to the synagogues in Damascus, so that if he found any there who belonged to the Way, whether men or women, he might take them as prisoners to Jerusalem. As he neared Damascus on his journey, suddenly a light from heaven flashed around him. He fell to the ground and heard a voice say to him, "Saul, Saul, why do you persecute me?" "Who are you, Lord?" Saul asked. "I am Jesus, whom you are persecuting," he replied. "Now get up and go into the city, and you will be told what you must do."

The men traveling with Saul stood there speechless; they heard the sound but did not see anyone. Saul got up from the ground, but when he opened his eyes he could see nothing. So they led him by the hand into Damascus. For three days he was blind, and did not eat or drink anything. In Damascus there was a disciple named Ananias. The Lord called to him in a vision, "Ananias!"

"Yes, Lord," he answered. The *Lord told him*, "Go to the house of Judas on Straight Street and ask for a man from Tarsus named Saul, for he is praying. *In a vision he has seen a man named Ananias come and place his hands on him to restore his sight.*" **"Lord," Ananias answered,** "I have heard many reports about this man and all the harm he has done to your saints in Jerusalem. And he has come here with authority from the chief priests to arrest all who call on your name."

But the Lord said to Ananias, "Go! This man is my chosen instrument to carry my name before the Gentiles and their kings and before the

people of Israel. *I will show him how much he must suffer for my name.*"
Then ***Ananias*** went to the house and entered it. Placing his hands on
Saul, he said, *"Brother Saul, the Lord—Jesus*, who appeared to you
on the road as you were coming here—has sent me so that you may see
again and be filled with the **Holy Spirit.**" Immediately, something like
scales fell from Saul's eyes, and he could see again. He got up and was
baptized, and after taking some food, he regained his strength.

Using God's Wisdom to Make Divine Relationship Adjustments

Moving from problems to privileges in relationships can prove to
be very difficult without proper instructions and guidance. Another wise
method that has helped me tremendously is the method of the four (4)
Ps which are: "Problems, Principles, Processes, and Privileges."

"Universal Principle"

Until you are aware of your problem, you will keep making the
same mistakes over and over again. Not only does the Kingdom way
help us identify our problems, but gives us firm methods and measures
that empower us to correct and change them if we submit to and obey;

Problem:

*Mark 10:13-16, Then they brought little children to Him, that He
might touch them; but the disciples rebuked those who brought them.
But when Jesus saw it, He was greatly displeased and said to them, "Let
the little children come to Me, and do not forbid them; for of such is the
kingdom of God. Assuredly, I say to you, whoever does not receive the*

kingdom of God as a little child will by no means enter it." And He took them up in His arms, laid His hands on them, and blessed them.

The Kingdom way teaches us that we should never in the slightest violate another *individual despite the position we may have with them or over them.* **Power we gain through manipulation and domination will eventually fail.**

Matthew 18:1-4 At that time the disciples came to Jesus, saying, "Who then is greatest in the kingdom of heaven?" Then Jesus called a little child to Him, set him in the midst of them, and said, "Assuredly, I say to you, unless you are converted and become as little children, you will by no means enter the kingdom of heaven. Therefore whoever humbles himself as this little child is the greatest in the kingdom of heaven. Whoever receives one little child like this in My name receives Me.

Principle:

Matt.6:33; But seek aim at and strive after first of all His Kingdom and His *righteousness His way of doing and being right*, and then all these things taken together will be given you besides.

Kingdom principles take an uncommon approach to power because they are based on principles, not practices. When you *understand* Kingdom principles, you can create effective practices. Which ultimately produce Christ-centric power?

Prov. 3:5 Trust God from the bottom of your heart; don't try to figure out everything on your own. Listen for God's voice in everything you do, everywhere you go; he's the one who will keep you on track.

Don't assume that you know it all. Run to God! Run from evil!

Your understanding and ability to apply what you are learning can transcend specific situations, people, and problems.

James 1:22, *"don't fool yourself into thinking that you are a listener when you are anything but, letting the Word go in one ear and out the other. Act on what you hear! Those who hear and don't act are like those who glance in the mirror, walk away, and two minutes later have no idea who they are, what they look like."*

"If you underestimate your power, you get inaction; if you overestimate it, you get conflict and antagonism. When you are clear about your power, you can increase it and do more good," in the words of Author Blaine Lee. This righteousness makes you more careful what you ask of others; because you are more likely to check your own motive first.

Process 3 stages:

I. Processing the Problem:

Trouble begins whenever we try to force fit people into space we occupy rather than accept them as they are, and if they can't accommodate us, move on.

II. Principle:

2 Cor. 6:14-18, WARNS all of us, do not make miss-mated (unsuited) alliances with those that are inconsistent with your faith!

Be careful how you develop a friendship with people whose influence is stronger than the principles that your life must be governed by. Principles reflect your internal core values.

III. Process:

"The Law of acceptance" –all things are lawful but not expedient" *Let people be who they are, without force.* Accept what you see, without manipulation, this way you will know who you are dealing with. Remember who you are in light of your internal vision, and stay disciplined to those values that make you competent and purposeful, by standing your ground against compromise, in spite of how they make you feel or how things appear momentarily; and move on. Refuse to give access to your heart.

Prudence point: Never change your conviction or compromise godly standards in order to please someone else rather than yourself. And never ask friends or partners to change for you if it is against their conviction. Jesus said, Matt. 7:12, *"Therefore, whatever you want men to do to you, do also to them, for this is the Law and the Prophets."*

Bullet-This will prevent you from falling in love with or befriending someone's potential.

Divine relationships are not designed to be rehabilitation centers. If you see yourself falling in love with someone or befriending someone in order to *"change"* them into the person you think they should be, stop! You aren't being a lover; you are playing God.

IV. Privilege:

Note. You will discover that "Destiny partners and Life- time

Partnerships" already have the desire to do and be many of the things that are consistent with *whom you are* and are already moving in that direction without your manipulations. [Remember The Three E's] **Relationships fail for 2 reasons:**

You are with the right person or persons, but don't know how to make the relationships work, or you are with the wrong person. (Problems arise because of inherent incompatibility). Keep your "Sexuality" under control while you are developing relationships of every sort.

Good Relations Require Givers and Takers

You must make it your priority to find people you can have healthy exchanges with without violating yourself!

If you do right by yourself, you will have plenty of time to express your sexuality according to the creators' design for it. God planned for "Singles" to help each other dominate and run the earth undistracted with the problems that only "Sex" can cause.

God ordained Sex for Married people. He also ordained Marriage for Responsible people, and Responsibility for Mature people. Mature people understand that when decisions are appropriated they determine Consequences. These mature persons willingly bear responsibility for their Actions without excessive cost to others.

Decisions to have Sex outside of God's will continue to permeate social irresponsibility and amplifies relationship pain. This is the primary reason you should commit to developing your relationships without sex.

Sex – Character - Skills = Divorce

You must understand that "GOOD SEX" does not require Character nor Relationship skills, but "GOOD RELATIONSHIPS" requires both. One reason divorce rates are so high is because "We master satisfying a person's body [3-15 min], but lack the ability to become an asset to their life.

In many cases those who SELL sex as a trade-off for relationship development, discover that all they PURCHASED is a Sex Partner who is able to "Perform" in bed, but has no skills for "Partnership".

"Partner vs. Performer"

In every marriage the goal should be to have a performance based partnership, yet the rush to enter into relationships without proper guidance is often due to a lack of restraint and self control. This is the single reason why you should abstain from sex before you are very familiar with the person you are considering as a **"Life-Time Partner"**. Sex before marriage distorts both "Perspective and Maturity" causing disillusionment about "Reality".

Actually the persons Character, practices and habits, goals and aspirations, friendships and associations are far more important foundationally than how good sex can be.

The things that are most important are their beliefs, standards, convictions and values about God, Family, Money, Work, Responsibilities, Pleasures, etc....

Before you consider entering into any kind of intimacy, especially "Life-Partnership" it is good to know some things about the person's family, how they relate to their parents and siblings, what they [person's family] think about the person you are considering, their credit report, how they manage their affairs, and how they deal with pressure and indifference. Understanding these characteristics will enhance the partner's ability to sustain the passion for partnership with longevity, thus setting the stage for great sex in marriage.

The "Playboy – Hustler" thrill is good only for dogs, hogs, and frogs who don't have to account for their actions. But, "we humans" have to live through our hearts. Which at some point will began to experience pain from animalistic behavior. You are not an animal; you are a precious child of God who needs to learn swiftly how to value yourself as more than a functional sex object.

Many have made the mistake of allowing their functional desires and ways of expressing their sensuality to define who they are sexually. This is tragic because originally **"sex" was not intended to be an issue of character definition** nor personal identity for singles.

When sex is put back in its original context and design immediately it will cease to be a problem causing function or habit in this society. Your sexuality is not your identity it is solely your gender. **You were born to be what your gender is** in spite of how you **desire** to express it, and in what context you choose marriage or single. Our desires are mainly shaped by exposure, imaginations and feelings, and suggestions. When we control these forces we are then better able to maintain correct posture with ourselves.

You had no decision in the matter of your gender, but what you do with and how you choose to express your gender is your choice for the rest of your life. Just remember, even though you do as you choose, you will not be able to determine the consequences or recompense for your actions.

Every individual's responsibility and accountability begins the very moment a person decides to carry out their desires within the context of the design of a thing or outside of its intended purpose.

Always remember that **"desires" expressed determine if a thing is pure or defile for the person expressing themselves.** Like all other things in this life that are either born or manufactured sex has its proper use and purpose.

Unequal Yokes (different beliefs)

2 Corinthians 6:14-18, **warns** us all,

Do not make miss-mated (unsuited) alliances with those that are inconsistent with your faith!

*Don't become partners with those who reject God. How can you make a partnership out of right and wrong? **That's not partnership; that's war.** Is a light best friend with dark? Does Christ go strolling with the Devil? Do trust and mistrust hold hands? Who would think of setting up pagan idols in God's holy Temple? But that is exactly what we are, each of us a temple in whom God lives. God himself put it this way: I'll live in them, move into them; I'll be their God and they'll be my people. So leave the corruption and compromise; leave it for good,"* *says God."**Don't link up with those who will pollute you.** I want you all for myself. I'll be a Father to you; you'll be sons and daughters to me." The Word of the Master, God. (The Message)*

The people you have around you most frequently are really important. Because your associations speak volumes to both where you are and the direction your life will take. Who do you spend the majority of your time with? You risk the possibility of becoming like what you are around. Make sure you spend a lot of time with God because the more you hang out with him the more you become like him.

We must use extreme caution as we select our frequent associations not to appear to be conceited or to good for people, but you don't want to be infected by wrong associations. Also be careful under what circumstances you formulate your alliances and intimate associations. The relational deceptions of your heart can become divisive in the hands of Satan during critical moments of your life.

You must begin to see life as a continual journey, a destination that you will travel throughout your "lifetime". This will enable you to become decisive about carrying the most significant and relevant personnel you possibly can. It will also allow you to make your journey as unencumbered and unhindered as possible.

Here are four Relevant Questions to assist you in making wise relational choices:

1. Who am I?

2. What is my purpose?

3. Where am I going?

4. Who is going with me?

There is a certain bias that you are supposed to walk in regarding your future with persons who will closely associate with you.

Becoming fit for relationships

Universal scriptural principles are designed to impact the total landscape of your life in relationships weather Single, Married, Friend, Parent, Partnership, Co-worker, Supervisors, etc. Matt.6:33 clearly state that we are to seek righteousness first. A good friend of mine, Bishop Ken Fuller always says **"Everything happens at the speed of Relationships."**

It is a good practice for every Kingdom citizen who truly wants solid relationships but just can't figure out how to create **"winning"** situations in every exchange. Without losing yourselves I want you to become suspicious of everything you've been taught about men and women before your new life began.

Erase the myths, the heresies, everything your credible relationships incorrectly told you, all the advice you've read in magazines and seen on television that disagrees with God's word. Continue to journey with me through scripture, and let's explore together what the creator who is our father has to say about "Relationships, their purpose, and the correct way to function in them."

Satan is counting on you continuing to get your advice from other sources who do not know his tactics or how he has shaped the mind-set of those persons you have to interact with in multiple ways, daily. All Believers must realize the need for Mind-Renewal before experiencing the abundant life and peace carved out for us in our relationships.

Notice Proverbs 4:10-26 (The Message), *Dear friend, take my advice; it will add years to your life. I'm writing out clear directions to Wisdom Way, I'm drawing a map to Righteous Road. I don't want you ending up in blind alleys, or wasting time making wrong turns. Hold tight to good advice; don't relax your grip. Guard it well—your life is at stake!*

Don't take wicked bypass; don't so much as set foot on that road. Stay *clear of it; give it a wide berth. Make a detour and be on your way. Evil people are restless unless they're making trouble; they can't get a good night's sleep unless they've made life miserable for somebody. Perversity is their food and drink, violence their drug of choice. The ways of right-living people glow with light; the longer they live, the brighter they shine. But the road of wrongdoing gets darker and darker— travelers can't see a thing; they fall flat on their faces.*

Learn It by Heart

Dear friend, listen well to my words; tune your ears to my voice. Keep my message in plain view at all times. Concentrate! Learn it by heart! Those who discover these words live really live; body and soul, they're bursting with health.

Keep vigilant watch over your heart; that's where life starts. Don't talk out of both sides of your mouth; avoid careless banter, white lies, and gossip. Keep your eyes straight ahead; ignore all sideshow distractions. Watch your step, and the road will stretch out smooth before you. Look neither right nor left; leave evil in the dust.

Let's Get Understanding About

Generational differences and Gender differences
between Men and Women

When we fail to understand how and why someone may be different than us, we are actually leaving a lot of room for conflict. Especially since "communication" is such a vital factor in all relationships.

It is very important that we use these insights to make us more effective in the process of growing in our relationships on every level. Dr. Willard Harley, a Christian psychologist, who directs a network of mental health clinics in Minnesota has interviewed thousands of couples over 25 years as a marriage counselor and discovered the 10 most important needs of husbands and wives.

They are discussed in his book, *His Needs/Her Needs*. He's identified 5 basic needs of women and 5 basic needs of men generally. Although the list may not apply to some relationships, let's see how the differences can be used to bring light to how we function many times in our relationships.

The five basic needs for men:
- ✔ Sexual fulfillment
- ✔ Recreational companionship
- ✔ An attractive spouse
- ✔ Domestic support
- ✔ Admiration

The five deepest needs of women:

- ✔ Affection
- ✔ Conversation
- ✔ Honesty and Openness
- ✔ Financial Security
- ✔ Family commitment

Notice these lists do not overlap anyplace? I use them to demonstrate that because those deepest needs of men and women, in general do not correspond there is conflict from the beginning. What happens many times in marriages is that men, knowing what their deepest needs are, figure a woman has those same needs. So he without hesitation attempts to meet the deepest needs he thinks she has. A woman knows her deepest needs and in turn does the same.

In either case the relationship will grow into conflict eventually unless their assumptions are replaced with a more personalized understanding of the individual they are married to.

Generational

In speaking about the evolution of relationships historically, it has become increasingly clear that it is also important for today's church to be informed about generational changes to remain knowledgeable. If we were to take a look at the people who attend church on Sunday we would see 41 percent are Baby Boomers, 30 percent fall within Generation X and 21 percent falls within the Millennial and only 8 percent are the Traditionalists. What makes this information so important? It becomes important when major decisions are being made regarding church programs, events and functions.

Sometimes the people making the decisions may not think to consider others, especially if the majority of the ones making the decisions fall into the same age or generational percentile. Each generation is necessary for the success of any church. Each has something to contribute.

These **four generations are constantly overlapping** in some fashion from soon to be retired from ministry to just getting saved and entering into ministry. The age gaps and how they are known help us to be better prepared to understand how to relate to the four generations.

Traditionalists were born before 1946, they are known as Veterans, WWII, Matures, Silent, Radio Age, Old School, etc. **The Baby Boomers** were born from 1946 to 1964 and are often described as the television age. **Generation X'ers** were born between 1965 and 1976 and known as the computer-age and Internet generation. The millennial generation was born between 1977 and 2000 are known as generation Y, who are the Internet and digital agers.

Traditionalist in church are often referred to as being set in their ways, not real adaptable to change. Sometimes they wish things were the way they used to be. **Baby Boomers** are optimistic, charismatic, like people who take charge, problem solvers, buy it now and pay for it later, change jobs/churches/companies every few years, not afraid to step and take a chance.

Generation X are cynical, value work and family balance, have faith in own ability, independent, straightforward, change is good, change jobs/church every two-three years if they don't feel fulfilled. **Millennial** outlook on life is optimistic, technological gadgets are prevalent, practical, create bonds with family or friends, environment friendly, bored easily, rotate jobs frequently, disinterested in church unless personally involved. The Millennial must be involved to attend on a consistent basis.

Gender

When we look at our gender differences it is a documented fact that every cell in a man's body is different than a woman's body. When we acknowledge this reality it accounts for many of the differences and frustrations that men and women experience daily while trying to communicate.

Chemicals flowing through our bodies are different. Muscle structure is different. Women have a better immune system and are stronger at conception. Fewer baby girls die than boys do. This usually averages out somewhere around when we're fifteen years of age.

Women also have fewer diseases because they are stronger physically at resistance of certain sicknesses and diseases. Someone suggested that "If it came down to it women would do better in concentration camps than men."

On the other hand men have 1,000,000 more red blood cells in every drop of blood. Men have more energy and can work longer. Men have 11/2 gallons of blood flowing through their body. Women have 4/5ths gallon of blood flowing.

Men's body is about 40 percent muscle weight. Women's body is about 20 percent. That's why most men can out arm-wrestle most women.

Women have a layering of insulating cells over their body that make women prettier. But it is easier for women to gain weight and harder to lose than Men.

Men's skin is thicker. Bones are heavier. I wonder if women know that a Man's skull is thicker.

Most fascinating "Differences"

A few days *after conception* mothers release a chemical. When it hits a girl nothing happens, but when it hits a boy it makes testosterone. It drives the man sexually, makes a Man aggressive, and changes a Man's body, causing his arms and legs to become more active.

When this same chemical hits the brain it washes the brain and makes Men lateral brained causing us to use *one part of the brain* at a time.

Women are bilateral which means they have more connecting fibers from one side of the brain to the other. They can use *both sides* of the brain at one time. Their intuition allows them to take in more information at any time.

Men favor the left side of the brain: logical side, language, engineering, and accounting. This is true for 80% of the men and 80% of the women. The left side is also cold, factual, and conquering.

Women favor the right side but use both. They feel, cry more easily, and always know how you feel. Sometimes better than you! A little humor.

It's also true in little children

Little girls are more talkative, little boys less talkative. What moves more significantly on a little girl right after birth are her lip muscles? This is why one of the greatest things women give us is intimate communication.

Men more aggressive, start more fights, and have more violent dreams. Women have more romantic dreams.

Men are harder to teach, have more problems reading, and are more argumentative. All of these differences can cause a strain on a relationship. Here are 5 **major differences** between men and women.

Five Major Communication Differences in Men and Women

1. Men tend to want to discover and express facts/Women want to express, intuition, and emotions.
2. Men need solutions/women love to give sympathy.
3. Men are more objective/Women are more emotional.
4. Men can separate themselves from their surroundings. Women tend to have a hard time separating themselves from their home, children, and jobs. Men commonly get their identity from what they do, women from who they know. Men see home as a resting place, not a place of work.
5. Men tend to generalize/women are more detailed. The average

woman can remember what someone did to her 10 years ago and what they were wearing when they did it.

Unforgiveness; a Signal of Love

Many times, unforgiveness is a position we retain towards people we really love, because we are not able to get what we want from them on our terms, in our time. Usually what we think we should or what we feel they owe us.

Sometimes we may even feel that someone or something else is getting the respect, honor, attention, fellowship, affection, recognition, position, privilege, time or reward we deserve.

When this happens both the appearance of, and the suspicions of things we sense based upon past experiences or what we are hearing, regardless of whether they are true or not, actually keeps the emotion and the imagination actively present to sustain the idea of pain, hurt, rejection, or loss. *"The spirit of a man sustains his infirmity."*

This disposition often turns into resentment because the hurtful experience is allowed to linger too long and at lengthy periods. We must remember that the Satan knows how to use our thoughts & feelings to keep a past experience alive as if it is present tense, so the trauma of an emotional imagination even though past, acts as real as an actual event that is present.

When we fail to stay conscious of this, Satan takes advantage of us through our ignorance giving us reasons to store and harbor unforgiveness in our memory bank (conscience) files. This exposes the reason we are commanded to forgive.

CHAPTER
11

Next I Must Understand

"MONEY"

Putting proactive measures in place

MY MONEY NEEDS A MISSION

"For wisdom is a defense, and money is a defense:"
"A feast is made for laughter, and wine makes merry: but money
answers all things."

Ecclesiastes 7:12; 10:19

King Solomon through the wisdom of God established the absolute
necessity of money in the earth realm, even for Kingdom citizens. Like
air, water, food, and love; money is an essential medium through which
life is lived, and in many cases it actually determines our freedom and
comfort in this life.

Sixteen of the thirty-eight parables recorded in the bible are about how to handle money. There are also more than **two thousand, three hundred and fifty verses** recorded in the scriptures about money and possessions. Only five hundred verses are recorded on prayer, and less than five hundred verses on faith, of the which, *"without faith it is impossible to please God."*

When we compare the documented mention of money, with the mention of other important issues recorded in the Bible, such as prayer and faith, to determine its' importance. It becomes obvious that a proper understanding of money, the right relationship with money, and the appropriate use of money, is how we bring balance and symmetry to our lives. This ultimately pleases God and allows us to fulfill our missions which should correspond with our purpose in the earth. Our money needs a mission.

This is the primary reason Believers must stop relegating finance and abundance to the bottom of their agenda. We cannot afford to continue feeling ambivalent about the financial part of our lives anymore. **These simultaneous conflicting feelings make you disinterested in the proper pursuit of financial prosperity because of your personal ignorance, and fear of persecution, which are sure to come from many of your religious friends.**

Jesus promised in the gospel of Mark, chapter 10:29-30, that the wealth and increase in the Kingdom, comes with persecution. Persecution is often what non-progressive religious and worldly people do, when their minds have been blinded by Satan, as a type of spiritual warfare to defeat the Kingdom of God through poverty permeated by impoverished minds.

Paul said, in his letter to the Ephesians, that their mind blindness remains because, *"their understanding is darkened, being alienated (estranged, self banished) from the life of God through the ignorance (the want of knowledge and perception, the willful blindness) that is in them, because of the blindness of their heart"*

This is what makes mind renewal and discipleship training so urgent after salvation. When we fail to become enlighten to the righteousness which makes one acceptable to God, in word, thought, and deed. We go about establishing our own righteousness based upon our ignorance and assumptions. And actually live our lives beneath the privilege of our heritage.

Notice Mark 10:29-30, *"Verily I say unto you, there is no man that has left house, or brothers or sisters or mother or father or children or lands for my sake and the gospel's. Who will not receive a hundredfold now in this time, houses, brothers, sisters, mothers, children, and lands,* **with persecutions** *and in the world to come eternal life.*

The persecution mentioned is not to provoke fear in Believers but, to acknowledge the confirmation of Godliness that results from what Satan meant as evil.

Money Answers and Defends

There are several ways that money both answers and defends us in our attempt to accomplish our purpose according to Solomon, in the book of Ecclesiastes: Money allows us to own our on time, to stop being preoccupied with survival so we may focus on God's agenda and

Kingdom missions, and having money frees us from money: It allows us to get on with our lives without fretting about money on a daily bases.

For many years in ministry I've observed frustrated Believers who desire to win souls, manifest their spiritual gifts, work in the mission fields, and do whatever they can to win the world for Christ. **But their inability to get beyond** bad doctrines and false teachings regarding money and biblical prosperity turns their desires into wish list that never manifest into reality.

It's a sad reality, but **their scriptural philosophy is too small to serve their God given desires, dreams, and aspirations.** *They rest and twist the scriptures to their own hurt."*

Having Money is Like Not Having a Toothache!

Someone once said, "When you have a toothache, all the other sensations and experiences in your life are put aside to deal with the nagging pain. Everything about you consciously is at the mercy of that one throbbing nerve. All you can think of is your tooth. Your tooth becomes your whole world. When the toothache goes away, life opens up again. Having money is like not having a toothache.

We are only begging exploitation when we take a servile, scared, excuse laden approach to our financial prosperity.

Our journey in the Kingdom began with a change in status that confirmed us as children of God by faith, who by adoption became Abraham's seed, and heirs according to the promise.

Which means that, like our Father, Abraham; *we are blessed to be a blessing.* This indicates that God wants His children to use their wealth to spread the gospel throughout the world.

People who educate themselves to take control of processes and systems that are available to enhance their management skills financially, change entire systems and communities in God's favor because they tap into the power of wealth.

Deuteronomy 8:18, illustrates that

"God gives us power to get wealth,
to establish His covenant with us."

I am determined to discuss this very important issue with you because often Christians have difficulty discussing what they need most. In spite of all the abuse and incorrect measures that you have either experienced or heard about this issue must be set in order in your new life or you will not be able to enjoy it consistently.

For several years after my born again experience, I continued to struggle financially. Even though I made a lot of money my financial intelligence was very shallow. Like many today who assume that faith in God will cover their financial blunders, I was growing weary as a result of my ignorance and neglect to read what the Bible said about money and possessions in the fine print.

All of my life I had heard in the church that "money was the root of all evil" so I believe that somehow this misinformation affected my ability to prioritize financial issues properly. After many years of faithfully living a life dedicated to God the one hurdle that kept causing difficulty in my life was my money management problems. I had yet to discover that the Kingdom of God is a realm driven by knowledge although it is empowered by the Spirit of God.

HERE IS A LIST OF SCRIPTURES THAT PROVE **"THE KINGDOM OF GOD IS A REALM DRIVEN BY KNOWLEDGE, EMPOWERED BY THE HOLY SPIRIT."** Matthew 6:33; Romans 10:1-3; Matthew 22:29; John 5:38-39; 8:31-32; 15:7-8; 20:9; Isaiah 5:13; Jeremiah 32:32-34; Daniel 11:32; 1 John 5:14-15, and 3 John 2-4.

Notice, Hosea 4:6 clearly states that God's people are destroyed for a lack of knowledge," not a lack of money, friends, opportunities, etc. This implies that every area a Christian lacks the knowledge of how God would handle or manage an issue will subject them to destruction.

Questions to help you start realignment

Where do you get your financial advice? Who or what source is responsible for your understanding of how to use money? Do you seek out the advice of experts, the instructions from the scriptures or do you trust that you already know enough to stay out of trouble?

Most likely your knowledge is from personal experience, talking to others and a very little from reading. Your sources of advice are important. Problems arise when you trust the wrong people to help or advise you without experience or education.

It is also wise to know what gets people in trouble so you can recognize and avoid the warning signs. Someone once said, **"Education is when you read the fine print, experience is what you get when you do not."** In Matthew 25:24-30, the unprofitable servant is a prime example of what happens when we operate out of assumption and ignorance, even with God's money.

In today's society it has become increasingly obvious that many Christians handle their finances as if money is not important to God nor is it necessary to sustain the economy of the Kingdom. During a recent poll some suggested that they thought that churches focus too much time on offerings. Some had even concluded that since God is spiritual and money is natural, the subject was not that important to God. But nothing could be further from the truth.

A close examination of the scriptures reveals that Jesus Himself referred to money frequently in his teachings. This is why after the new birth experience mind renewal should began immediately so that a believer's opinions and perspectives can be realigned to the word of God for the sake of understanding and obeying God's will. As Pastor Greg Powe of Revealing Truth Ministries states "You must increase your financial IQ in order to succeed financially."

Let's set the record straight [Again!]

The Bible records 500 verses on prayer, less than 500 on faith, and an alarming 2,350 verses on money and possessions. In the Gospels alone, one out of every ten verses relates directly to the subject of money, that's one-tenth. Sixteen of the thirty-eight parables are concerned with the handling of money and possessions. Matthew 22:29 points out that "we error when we don't know the scripture, nor the power of God".

Clearly, God does care about money management as much He

cares about all of the other issues of our lives, so He has given us in His word, the blueprint for the proper stewardship of our finances.

I am praying that you will read, re-read, and meditate prayerfully each scriptural lesson we share, so that you may begin advancing through your commitment to obey Kingdom principles as we do. You must remember that *"Jesus came that you might have life and that more abundantly, so He wants you to prosper and be in health as your soul prospers."*

LET'S TAKE CONTROL OF OUR FINANCIAL FUTURES TOGETHER!

Now, for the record if you are going to live your life successfully as a child of God you must start by getting the foundation right. Remember that Jesus said we must dig deep before we begin lying or setting the stones in place. Often what we do as Kingdom citizens is set stones by assumption or simply without any regard for what we are doing.

This kind of living cannot be tolerated by God's children any longer because we have a calling on our lives to be *"The light of the world and the Salt of the earth"* which demands or operations and applications are aligned correctly with Truth.

BUILDING YOUR FINANCES ON THE RIGHT FOUNDATION

Psalm 11:3, *"if the foundations are destroyed. What can the righteous do?"*

What is a foundation and why is it important to have a foundation? Webster defines it as the base on which something rest; specif., the supporting part of a wall, house, etc., and at least partially underground, the fundamental principle on which something is founded. Basis; It is also a supporting material or part beneath an outer part, as a foundation garment.

Jesus stated in Matthew 13:35, "that it might be fulfilled which was spoken by the prophet, saying: *"I will open My mouth in parables; I will utter things kept secret from the foundation of the world."* Isn't it interesting that God has kept some "foundational things" secret although they are the base and fundamental principles on which things both in heaven and earth rest?

Notice how the Message Bible addresses the importance of a right foundation in Luke 6:48-49, **"If you work the words into your life**, *you are like a smart carpenter who dug deep and laid the foundation of his house on bedrock. When the river burst its banks and crashed against the house, nothing could shake it; it was built to last. But if you just use my words in Bible studies and don't work them into your life, you are like a dumb carpenter who built a house but skipped the foundation. When the swollen river came crashing in, it collapsed like a house of cards. It was a total loss."*

The Amplified further clarifies the need for right foundation, **"He is like a man building a house,** *who dug and went down deep and laid a foundation upon the rock; and when a flood arose, the torrent broke against that house and could not shake or move it, because it had been securely built or founded on a rock.* **But he who merely hears and**

does not practice doing My words is *like a man who built a house on the ground without a foundation, against which the torrent burst, and immediately it collapsed and fell, and the breaking and ruin of that house was great."*

The book of 1 Chronicles 29:11- 14, begins the introduction of the first two of four essential foundational principles that will assist the believer in establishing the correct attitude about God and money. They are in this order, 1. God owns 2. God controls 3. God provides 4. God requires our obedience.

First, **God Owns:** *"For all that is in heaven and in earth is yours"*. This knowledge establishes God as possessor of all things to free individuals from the wrong perspective concerning money and possessions.

Second, **God Controls:** *"For all things come from You* [God] *,"* (verse 14). Here we are reminded that God has set rules and principles in place to govern the affairs of men. Understanding this should convey confidence through trust which allows an individual to rest in God's promises when facing fear producing concerns over financial matters.

Third, **God Provides:** "For your heavenly Father knows that you need all these things" Matthew 6:32. Jehovah Jireh [God] has already promised to provide for all of our needs if we trust Him without doubting or worrying. See Philippians 4:19

Fourth, **God Requires Obedience:** *"Therefore whoever hears these sayings of Mine, and does them, I will liken him to a wise man who built his house on a rock"* Matthew 7:24.

Our obedience to the financial principles of the Lord who Owns,

Controls, and Provides is the final stone to be set in place to ensure our prosperity. We must renounce our ownership and independent ways, and commit ourselves to becoming good stewards of what God has entrusted to our care.

A Faithful Steward

Let's begin by defining a faithful steward. The word **"steward"** means manager, overseer, or supervisor. A steward is one entrusted with the responsibility of handling and administering the property and business of his master.

Faithful stewardship of finances requires more than just how much we give. It involves the proper management of all of the money and possessions God has entrusted to us.

God requires the same from all of His children, whether you have much or little. As I mention earlier in Matthew 25 God expected the man with one talent to obey the same principles the man who received five talents had to obey. Here we understand why Paul expressed to the Corinthians that *"Moreover it is required in stewards that one be* **found faithful"** 1Corinthians 4:2.

The implications are strong and weighty because they demonstrate God's forwardness to reward stewards according to their faithfulness to His demands in spite of their ignorance, neglect, or wrong attitude.

How We Handle Money Reveals Our Priorities and Values

What they reveal determines how God responds to us!

In other words we determine by our response to God's word how He will respond back to our needs. Matthew 6:24 tell us that "we cannot serve God and mammon". A faithful steward is an individual who has chosen to make financial decisions according to the word of God in spite of the shifts and circumstances that occur from day to day.

Observe closely the words of Jesus in Luke 16:11 notice His emphasis *"Therefore if you have not been faithful in the unrighteous mammon,* **who will commit to your trust the true riches?**" It is obvious that God grants spiritual blessing and favor upon us according to our faithfulness and integrity in financial matters.

After delivering Israel from Egypt, God established an ethical system to serve as the foundation for their nation. In it, He developed the laws of liability, restitution, and justice. He upheld honesty and integrity, and denounced stealing and covetousness.

The Christian must endeavor to maintain a good conscience before God and others in all of his business and financial matters. **"We must avoid the selfish and worldly tendency to advance our financial position through unscrupulous and dishonest practices.** This includes any form of cheating, deceitfulness, fraudulence, or unlawful behavior."

Though we may fool others, we cannot fool God. Remember, *"Whatever a man sows, that he will also reap"* Galatians 6:7.

John 10:10, which denotes a purpose for Jesus coming, is another great passage to clarify because of the absence of important foundational understanding in the lives of many regarding prosperity and Kingdom economics. Clearly the thief has done a masterful job by deceiving the masses about the need to take advantage of principles that yield increase for all Believers who participate.

The Bible must be seen as a book of applications not just a book of information, since "faith without works is dead". Also, it must be clear as we proceed that, in the words of Jesus, *"You do error, not knowing the scriptures, nor the power of God",* Matthew 22:29. A statement which implies that, limitation of knowledge is submission to error. I say this especially, regarding the understanding and use of the "Will of God". In this case a wrong application could lead to devastating consequences.

God is not obligated to perform nor bless our interpretations, although, He does honor and confirm the right applications with manifestations. Jeremiah 1:12, and Isaiah 55:11, together imply that God "hastens to perform" the correct appropriations of each word or principle He has sent and established. Simply stated, *"God's children are destroyed and are perishing because of a lack of knowledge".*

Satan knows that if the children of the Kingdom begin to appropriate the principles God put in place, like the children of the world respond to worldly methods. The ability of God would be prevalent in ministry because of the overflowing resources available to finance the demands of ministry to spread the gospel and expand the Kingdom throughout the world.

This is why Paul states in 2 Corinthians 4:3-4, *"But if our gospel be hid, it is hid to them that are lost: For the **god of this world** has blinded the unbelievers' minds that they should not discern the truth, preventing them from seeing the illuminating light of the Gospel of the glory of Christ, who is the image and likeness of God."*

Keep in mind that scriptural truths such as this; are for the discernment and the advancement of born again believers who have received the Holy Spirit into their hearts through salvation. *"And Jesus said to them, **To you** it has been given to know the mystery of the kingdom of God; but **to those** who are **outside**, all things come in parables, so that seeing they may see and not perceive, and hearing they may hear and not understand; Lest they should turn, And their sins be forgiven them,"* Mark 4:11-12.

Also, 1 Corinthians 2:14, *"But the natural, non-spiritual man does not accept or welcome or admit into his heart the gifts and teachings and revelations of the Spirit of God. For they are folly (foolishness, meaningless, non-sense) to him; and he is incapable of knowing them because they are spiritually discerned and estimated and appreciated."*

It is extremely important for me to list this point because Jesus candidly stated to Nicodemus in the gospel of John 3:1-12, that this is the single reason why his understanding of the miracles which denote the operation of God, was darkened and unable to grasp Kingdom measures.

More Proof God Wants To Prosper You

In the Old Testament; beginning with the book of Genesis, 17:1, God identified Himself for the first time, as the "Almighty God", which in the Hebrew is "El- Shaddai," God-all-sufficient or the God who is more than enough. In verse 2, the Almighty God or El-Shaddai made a covenant with Abram to **multiply** him exceedingly. This covenant is a reiteration of the promise God made to Abram in Genesis 12:2, which in essence is the offspring of the heritage of Genesis 1:28.

Notice *"And God blessed them, and said unto them, be fruitful and **multiply**."* Isaac called Jacob and pronounced a blessing upon him before sending him to the house of Bethuel to take a wife from the daughters of Laban, saying, *"And God Almighty bless thee, and make thee fruitful and **multiply** thee."* Genesis 28:1-3

In Genesis 35:11, God appeared to Jacob as he was returning to Bethel and said, *"I am God Almighty: be fruitful and **multiply**"*

Also Leviticus 26:3-9; Deuteronomy 7:13; and 8:1, 13; each list conditions that was required in order for Israel to **increase and multiply**. But, in Deuteronomy 8:18, God states emphatically, to Israel, *"That you shall remember the Lord your God, for it is He who gives you power to get wealth, that He may establish His covenant which He swore to your fathers."* Power implies multiply ways.

In the New Testament Jesus instructed Believers to give and harvest which is **increase and multiplication** shall be given back to you according to the measures you deal out; notice, Luke 6:38, *"Give, and it shall be given unto you; **good measure**, pressed down, shaken together, and running over, (in abundance) shall men give into your bosom. For with the same measure that you mete (when you confer benefits on others) withal it shall be measured to you again."*

In this we know that all harvest (reaping) is abundant, yet, often we forget that the proportion (size) of the harvest is always determined by the hand of the giver. Hence, the sower determines the harvest size.

God Supplies Givers so They Have Seed for Sowing

Both Isa. 55:10, and II Cor. 9:10, implies that, *"God who supplies* *seed for the sower and bread for eating will also provide and **multiply*** *your resources for sowing."*

It is increasingly obvious from these passages that the **Almighty God** known as El-Shaddai intends for His children to **increase and multiply** in a variety of ways. 3 John 2, records, *"Beloved, I pray above all things that you may prosper in every way and that your body may keep well, even **as your soul prospers**."*

In fact, Ecclesiastes 5:9, actually states that, *"the profit of the earth is for all."* Together these scriptures make two irreversible, irrefutable, self-confirming points that I have witnessed in demonstration throughout the world:

First, there are many diligent persons in both systems that enjoy the extravagant comforts of the earth, because they are consistent, and unrelenting in their pursuit of an enriched life of abundance. *"The thoughts of the diligent tend only to plenteousness."*

I'm speaking here about those who consistently use correct measures for advancement without any deviations from what is honest, right, and ethically required of them.

These diligent persons abound with blessings according to established principles and, therefore, should be commended rather than persecuted, or admired rather than despised. (Mark 10:29-30; 1 Peter 4:12-16; Hebrews 6:7-12)

Second, there are multitudes of slothful persons who remain without earth's comforts because they are bound to slothfulness, complacency and wrong practices through ignorance, which alienates them from the life that God intends for them to enjoy. A point that must be clarified because, "it is not God's will that any should perish." (Proverbs 10:4-5; 12:11, 24; 13:18; 21:5; and Ephesians 4:17-18).

How the "Grace" of God abounds

*Next, let's discuss the way that the grace of God abounds in the lives of Believers so that you may realize two important things: **1.** How much control and influence you do have upon your own prosperity and financial or economic advancement. **2.** How to make it work for you. Keep in mind that God has given you Salvation, but you must work it out.

Note, The main point of this discussion is to demonstrate the fact that the will of God is not automatic, but requires participation and cooperation for advancement.

2 Corinthians 9:6-8, states plainly, *"Remember this: he who sows sparingly and grudgingly will also reap sparingly and grudgingly, and he who sows bountifully and generously shall also reap bountifully and generously. Let everyone give as he has made up his own mind and purposed in his heart, not grudgingly (reluctantly) or of necessity (sorrowfully or under compulsion), for God loves a cheerful (joyous, "prompt to do it") giver, whose heart is in his giving.*

And God is able to make all grace (every favor and earthly blessing) abound toward you or come to you in abundance; so that you may always and under all circumstances and whatever the need, be self sufficient; possessing enough to require no aid or support and furnished in abundance for every good work and charitable donation." (KJV, AMP)

"God is able", but, just because God (the almighty, all sufficient one) is able; or God has the ability to do all, every, and anything, does not mean, God will! So then how to make all grace abound towards me is another issue, in spite of God's ability.

We quote John 10:10, frequently, but do all saints have abundance? Are all Believers living in streams that are overflowing? Or is it safe to say that Born again Believers have "access by faith into this grace where in we stand, that they have not taken advantage of because of wrong interpretations, and wrong expectations based upon false information? Clearly the scriptures illustrate that, "God watches over His word to perform it, not wrong interpretations".

Another point of emphasis is that, the Almighty God through your participation, according to what you purpose to offer, or give, is able to give you increase and multiplication in two forms:

1. All sufficiency   2. Abundance

*Sufficiency is for daily demands and Abundance is for extra demands that are above your normal, or the routine challenges of your existence. Again remember; what, when, where, and how you sow determines the similitude of you harvest. Not God moving automatically to give you increase and multiplication.

These principles that I am setting before you denote that, *"God gives you the power to get wealth,"* not automatic endowments of wealth and increase for your existence without your participation. In other words, as we appropriate these principles by faith they eventually yield optimum returns. So keep this in mind,

*God's ability is controlled by your ability!

God's Stewards and What He Expects From Them

Another important point of emphasis that needs to be considered is How God views Stewards and what He expects from them. In the gospel of Matthew 25:14-30, Jesus used the "parable of the Talents" to illustrate the Kingdom of Heaven's perspective about profitable and unprofitable stewards.

"For the kingdom of heaven is as a man travelling into a far country, who called his own servants, and delivered unto them his goods. And unto one he gave five talents, to another two, and to another one; to every man according to his several ability; and straight way took his journey.

Then he that had received the five talents went and traded with the same, and made them other five talents. And likewise he that had received two, he also gained two talents more. But he that had the one went and dug a hole in the ground and hid his Lord's money.

Now after a long time the master of those servants returned and settled accounts with them. And so he that had five talents came and brought him five more, saying, Lord you entrusted to me five talents; see, I have gained five talents more. His lord said unto him, well done, you good and faithful servant: thou has been faithful over a few things, I will make you ruler over many things: enter into the joy of your Lord.

He also that received two talents came and said, Lord, you entrusted me with two talents; behold, I have gained two other talents beside them. His Lord said unto him, well done, good and faithful servant; you have been faithful and trustworthy over a few things, I will make you ruler over many things: enter into and share the joy of your Lord.

Then he which had received the one talent came and said, Lord,

*I knew you to be a hard man, reaping where you did not sow, and gathering where you have not strawed: And I was afraid, and went and hid your talent in the earth: Here you have what is your own. But his Lord answered and said unto him. You wicked and slothful servant, you knew that I reap where I have not sowed and gather where I have not strawed: Then you should have **put my money** to the exchangers, and then at my coming I would have received **what was my own** with usury. Take therefore the talent from him, and give it to the one who has the ten talents.*

For unto everyone who hath (who puts my part to the exchangers) will more be given, and he shall have abundance: but from him that hath not shall be taken away even that which he hath.

Notice, the profitable stewards increased abundantly, but, the unprofitable steward lost what he had to the most profitable steward.

Principle: *God does not give more to slothful, excuse filled, stewards but is willing [to give more to those who increase using appropriate measures for exchange **with His part.**

Principle: *God will take from neglectful, slothful, unprofitable stewards and give what they do not exchange properly (both **His part and their part**) to a steward who increases mightily by obeying His will.

*Here, I think it is proper to note the emphasis of **Isaiah 55:10**, "that it (the word God sent) may **give seed** to the sower", and **2 Corinthians 9:10**, "And **God** who *provides seed* for the sower... and multiply your seed sown, and increase the *fruits* of your righteousness."

• **Notice what happened to the widow who gave**

God's part to His representative first:

In 1 Kings 17:13, Elijah instructed the widow during the famine too, "make me a little cake of *it *first,* and bring it to me, and afterwards prepare some for yourself and your son. * She took the first of "it", (the cake) and gave to the Prophet first.

Verses 15-16, "She did as Elijah said, and *she*, and *he,* and *her household* ate for <u>many</u> days. The jar of meal was **not spent** nor did the bottle of oil fail, according to the word which the Lord spoke through Elijah. *Notice the progression of the miracle from sufficiency to abundance:

• The Widow mentioned only two persons that she seemed to have regarded in the eating of the last meal, her and her son.

• The Prophet who is God's representative instructed her to ***fearnot**, *prepare to feed the **kingdom's** representative **first**, *from it (the cake), and *bring it to him, (offer **the first part** of "it" to God) and *afterward prepare some for yourself and your son. *Note, all first things belong to God as an act of worship, or we could say, the first part of all things belongs to the source we honor above all others.

• Then *the Lord declared out of the mouth of the Prophet that the "jar of meal shall not waste, or the bottle of oil fail.

• *She obeyed the word of the Lord, (the source she decided to acknowledge as first). Which in this case the source she worshiped with her first part (the Almighty God) assumed responsibility for sustaining her and her household throughout the famine. (Deuteronomy 20:20)

• See the progression. Neither the meal in the jar nor the oil in the bottle could fail **"until"**; so she and he and ***her household** (family and servants) ate for many days. Her entire household ate out of the **abundance**. The meal and the oil abundantly supplied them all. Her abundance became her households' sufficiency, because she moved from not enough, to more than enough abundance in one exchange.

• "If we are willing and obedient we shall also eat the good of the land". I firmly believe that it is God's desire to *"supply all of our need according to His riches in glory by Christ Jesus"* (Philippians 4:19).

My rule of thumb: Any time the **wisdom of God** draws attention to something it must take precedence over all other ways and methods because "Wisdom" *is the principle thing* or the method of formation, operation, or procedure exhibited in a given instance. In this case it is a principle method of Kingdom operation that God has prequalified for our use.

Webster regards anything considered as "the principle thing," the fundamental law or an essential part. Hence, the implication of Proverbs 3:9 strongly emphasizes the need for all Kingdom citizens to make the inclusion of this principle an essential part of our systematic way of "Honoring the Lord" each year. As I proceed here are several points you should remember from verses 9 and 10:

1. It is a mistake (against God's wisdom) to think that giving will in any way make us poor. Actually giving for God's honor is the most likely way to make us rich.

2.   As citizens of the Kingdom, we must be ruled in everything by God's will.

3.   There is no greater enemy to the fear of God in our hearts, than the conceitedness of our own wisdom.

4.   We must take heed of doing anything to offend God and forfeit His divine care.

5.   Psalm 24:1, states that not only does God own the earth, but everything and everyone who lives in it. See, 1 Chronicles 29:11-12; Psalm 50:10-12; Haggai 2:8. Isn't it safe to say that if we belong to Christ, it's logical that everything we have belongs to Him.

6.   "Where riches increase usually we are tempted to honor ourselves; but the more God gives us the more we should study to honor Him." Deuteronomy 8:17

7.   God who is first and best, must have the first and best of everything; He must be served first.

The promise in verse 10, illustrates that the surest and safest way of thriving and increasing little into much is in this principle. *"God shall bless you with increase."*

Now, to address why Money Needs Mission

A few years ago I carried a small group of discipleship students out to share their faith and witness in the community. While there we had a brief encounter with a homeless person who asked for a sizeable sum to invest in his habit and buy some food.

The student pointed the individual to me for a response. So I politely asked, Sir, what was the purpose you said you need money for? His reply was boldly stated and for my class very educational. I need some food and enough money to get some ___! Moved by his forwardness, I replied Sir, food we would gladly assist you with, but to your other request, my money has no such mission.

To underscore his point, he stated that he thought "we were real Christians who would appreciate his honesty." Then he proceeded to reprimand us for not doing what a "real" Christian would do. Unable to reach a compromise, he declined our food assistance and refused to entertain our witness any longer.

Unfortunately, this story is a reflection of many sad situations in our society. Multitudes of both Christians and non Christians fail to advance in their use of money because their "money has no mission."

Money without a mission is like Time without an assignment. We use it until it becomes a snare to us through our ignorance and abuse of it. Again I quote, "abuse is inevitable when we don't know the purpose of a thing." Haven't you noticed that without assigning a specific mission for your money you waste and spend out of control?

If you are in any way like I was the more money I made the more "debt" I accumulated. In other words I used money to buy debt, which is "Bondage" in every since of the word. I thought I was buying enjoyment, thrill, pleasure, and luxury. But I discovered after being haunted by bill collectors and pressing needs that I purchased worry, sadness, discomfort, and pain. I mean constant pain with a capital "P".

At one point I was in so much pain and constant pressure from bad debts that I could no longer enjoy going to work. It seemed like although I was making a lot of money, it was never enough because "The Bondage Exactor", I called him was already making plans for what my family and I were suppose to use for our advancement in the kingdom and the world

"Money with a Mission"

Imagine what will happen when the "children of God" do with money what "McDonald's and Wendy's and Kentucky Fried Chicken" are doing all over the world. We can actually take back the planet for the Kingdom of God!

This would mean:

- No more being hoodwinked by hidden-charges on credit cards
- No more feeling intimidated by financial institutions and the IRS
- No more struggling to survive year after year
- No more watching or envying others who enjoy the finer things in life

People have many problems dealing with money, because of the following reasons:

- impulse spending
- careless budgeting
- living beyond one's means
- credit problems
- constant borrowing from friends
- un-effective savings plans
- Extra jobs to pay all the bills at the expense of Marriage and Family time.

A famous bumper sticker reads, *"I can't be overdrawn, because I still have checks left!"*

God intended for money to be a blessing to us and others, but you must adapt to the Kingdom way, *"Give and it will be given to you"* (Luke 6:38) In fact, the Paul said that the problem isn't money, it's the *love of money* that is "a root of all kinds of evil" (1 Timothy 6:10). Most of us would certainly agree that we need to be in control of our finances. By saving money, keeping cost down, and having the ability to fulfill our desires without setbacks.

The problem of our financial outgo exceeding our input is due to a lack of "structure" When we have difficulty saying no to spending more than we should, we run the risk of becoming someone else's servant: *"The rich rule over the poor, and the borrower is servant to the lender."* (Proverbs. 22:7)

Here are a few tips that helped me to change MY dilemma:

"The Big <u>Three</u> Guidelines to Abundance"

By Christian author, Tessa Albert Warschaw, Ph.D.

1. Start by letting your satisfactions determine your Lifestyle Priorities and make trade-offs on the basis of that.

   o What do you Love and need most in your life?

   o You will never fulfill your agenda for abundance if it's something you don't want to do.

   o Listen to your feelings before you embark on a cause of action align with the Word

   o Change habits to fuel your agenda for abundance (strip off dead-weight)

2. Tear down the wall of ignorance and educate yourself:

- o Educate yourself about money: how it operates in your life and in the world
- o Take courses, attend seminars, brokerage houses & banks, and buy books.
- o Arrange a mentorship from the most conscious money person you know.
- o Work at developing money articulation like learning a new language
- o Fight "apathy" ignorance of money is a habit you can kick.

3. Follow the money. (Two things you need)

- o Find out in what fields, what industries, and what parts of the country the Money is in.
- o Then try to marry or merge your interest with it
- o Do research, read futurist magazines: Omni, The Future, Forbes, Fortune, and the Wall Street Journal.

Courses are also offered by the "Securities Training Institute"

"THE DEBT TRAP"

I mentioned earlier that in Proverbs 22:7, wisdom teaches that *"The rich rules over the poor, And the borrower is servant to the lender."* (NKJV)

Notice how the Message Bible records it *"The poor are always ruled over by the rich, so **don't borrow and put yourself under*** *their power.*

Today, FINANCIAL DEBT is so common place in society that it is accepted as the norm rather than the exception. Buy now and pay later is the most advertised lifestyle viewed in every form of the world's media. But the bible warns against debt because it subjects an individual to the demands of others rather than God.

Planning Your Financial Mission

Financial planning is not just about a budget or investing. Rather it is a thinking process that helps achieve goals. Most people don't plan to fail. They simply fail to plan. A financial plan can be an important tool in helping achieve goals and dreams.

Your Five-step Financial Planning Process begins with: **Setting Goals** which are the foundation for plans and actions and should correspond with your core values be personally meaningful and clearly written.

Analyze information by gathering information to provide a map of where you've been, where you are now, and where and how you desire to go in the future.

Create a Plan to assist you in putting important pieces of a puzzle together. Implement the Plan by taking action your dreams become a reality. Monitor and Modify the Plan as life changes. Periodic reviews and revisions will be necessary as changes occur.

Remember that financial planning is an ongoing thinking process, not just an event or a product. Next, the ability to distinguish the difference between a need and a want is an important skill that you must develop as soon as you possibly can.

Another factor that weighs heavily in financial decision making is your personal values. They will have tremendous impact an influence on your financial directions and mission you will establish.

Since your goals will provide your personal plans and actions towards your financial accomplishments, you may want to use the acronym "SMART goals," to set up memorable perimeters.

"SMARTa Goals

S = Specific

M = Measurable

A = Attainable

R = Realistic

T = Time-bound

Your goals should also consist of three phases:

Short-term (up to three months)

Intermediate-term (between three months and one year)

Long-term (more than a year)

To further develop the discipline of "money with a Mission" you will need to keep a Personal Spending Record to document your income and spending on a chart to help you develop a budget. Keep this part of the process simple to avoid seeing it as a burden or distraction.

CHAPTER
12

My Faith Needs a Definite Aim and Chief Goal

I MUST UNDERSTAND "FAITH"

"Like the arrow shot from the bow of an archer, I must learn to Aim my Faith at the Promises of God and spiritual postures and so that I may use it as a server."

"Striving for a Crown"

It's interesting how the apostle Paul was careful to emphasize the importance of definite aims and chief goals for faith throughout his epistles. Seemingly the Believers of his generation were struggling much like today's generation regarding the appropriate use of faith. In his appeal to the Believers at Corinth notice how the Holy Spirit inspired his selection of words mainly to insight the importance of *discipline by conformance* to a specific purpose.

"Do you not know that those who run in a race all run, but one receives the prize? **Run in such a way that you may obtain it**. *And*

*everyone who competes for the prize is temperate in all things. Now they do it to obtain a perishable crown, but we for an imperishable crown. Therefore **I run thus: not with uncertainty**. Thus I fight: **not as one who beats the air**. But I discipline my body and bring it into subjection, lest, when I have preached to others, I myself should become disqualified."* (1 Corinthians 9:24-28)

Also to the Philippians' he emphasized the importance of Pressing toward the Goal for the sake of obtaining the prize by being consumed with a distinct purpose driven by preselected, vision drafted measures and behaviors.

*"Not that I have already attained, or am already perfected; but **I press on, that I may lay hold of that for which Christ Jesus has also laid hold of me**. Brethren, I do not count myself to have apprehended; but one thing I do, forgetting those things which are behind and reaching forward to those things which are ahead, **I press toward the goal for the prize** of the upward call of God in Christ Jesus."* (Philippians 3:12-14)

Point is that faith without vision (God-inspired revelation) is blind faith. Faith needs vision like eyes need sight. Without it neither can distinguish directionally what the more appropriate route or what the most important priority should be.

I like the way in which the twelfth chapter of Genesis unfolds because it reveals that whenever Heaven attempts to communicate or reveal something to an earthly or human agency, it has to be stated and repeated several times before the limited earthly mind can conceive or discern the heavenly intent.

"Now the LORD had said to Abram: "Get out of your country,

From your family And from your father's house, To a land that I will show you. I will make you a great nation; I will bless you And make your name great; And you shall be a blessing. I will bless those who bless you, And I will curse him who curses you; And in you all the families of the earth shall be blessed. So Abram departed as the LORD had spoken to him, and Lot went with him. And Abram was seventy-five years old when he departed from Haran."

Several important truths are revealed in these passages but the main emphasis related to this point is that first, Abram's faith began as the will of God for him was revealed to him.

Second, this revelation became the catalyst of his lifetime pursuit and personal mission for life.

Like Noah, who was given his assignment through vision to build an Ark that took over a hundred years to accomplish, both patriarchs were filled with a passion for the culmination of their destinies because their faith in God was driven and sustained by a directional purpose or prophetic promise. The absence of this foundational measure may serve as the main reason many in the body of Christ are stuck, struggling, and stymied in their daily attempts to please God, their Faith lacks a definite aim or a chief goal.

Let's look briefly at what faith is and how Jesus said it must be used in order to advance the Kingdom citizen. To begin let's establish that the **Law of Faith** is activated by repentance, affirmed by obedience, comes by hearing, and begins where the will of God is known and appropriated.

Romans 10:17 illustrates "The **source of faith** which comes by hearing the word of God." This is what Jesus was implying when he stated in Matthew 4:4 that *"It has been written, Man shall not live and be upheld and sustained by bread alone, but by every word that comes forth from the mouth of God."*

Romans 12:3 makes it clear that God has dealt to every man **The Measure of faith.** Galatians 5:22 reveals the **Fruit of Faith** which provides character. The **Word of Faith** in Romans 10:8 is for nourishment. In Heb 4:1-2 the apostle made it clear that the word of faith is profitable to us only when or if we mix what we hear with faith. Notice, *"Therefore, since a promise remains of entering His rest, let us fear lest any of you seem to have come short of it. For indeed the gospel was preached to us as well as to them; but **the word which they heard did not profit them, not being mixed with faith** in those who heard it."*

The Law of Faith mentioned in Romans 3:27 is for the regulation of the new life of the kingdom citizen, the **Gift of Faith** in 1 Corinthians 12:9 is given to us for the supernatural, and the **Spirit of Faith** in 2 Corinthians 4:13 provides fervency. Notice how it is stated, "And *since we have the same spirit of faith,* according to what is written, *"I believed and therefore I spoke,"* we also believe and therefore speak" implying the importance of our duplication of His methods.

The multiple and diverse **Results of Faith** in Hebrews 11 gives us illustrated proof of the broadness of the functional operation of faith. It also demonstrates the relevance or importance of its inclusion in all our affairs and exchanges when it is employed to assist and serve us in every situation. "Whatsoever is not of faith is sin."

Next, the **Trial of Faith** according to 1 Peter 1:7 keeps us close to God. **The End of Faith** mentioned in 1 Peter 1:9 is for the salvation of souls, the **Prayer of Faith** according to James 5:14 will save the sick, and the **Fight of Faith** in 1 Timothy 6:12 is supposed to be a *"good fight"* because we "put on the **Shield of Faith** to quench all fiery darts."

After we are convinced that a promise is for us we must believe that God means all he says about it and agree to all its truth without discounting any aspects of it. Here *Belief* is the trigger of faith.

1John 5:14 address how belief is converted into faith thru confidence, which signals a firm agreement between our emotions, imaginations or thoughts, and intellect based upon spiritual or natural evidence. *"And this is the confidence (the assurance, the privilege of boldness) which we have in Him: [we are sure] that if we ask anything (make any request) according to His will **(in agreement with His own plan)**, He listens to and hears us. And if (since) we [positively] know that He listens to us in whatever we ask, we also know [with settled and absolute knowledge] that we have [granted us as our present possessions] the requests made of Him."*

The Amplified version of Hebrews 11:1 also establishes this understanding that demands **conformance** from the **will, intellect,** and **dispositions** of the soul along with the thoughts and emotions. *"NOW FAITH is the assurance (the confirmation, the title deed) of the things [we] hope for, being the proof of things [we] do not see and the conviction of their reality [faith perceiving as real fact what is not revealed to the senses]."* Since it is not revealed to our natural senses an adjustment to spiritual logic and discernment in the entirety of the soul must be made to reinforce the belief to align with and take its cue from the *"perception of faith."*

I do believe that the most central part of the five faculty of the soul which makes this transition possible is the interior "intellect." The conversation that is more dominant or abundant in the heart is the dictator of the posture of the soul. When we take our cue from nature (external matters) our senses use carnal reasoning to validate and justify our responses. Thus any man whose internal dialect is bad will always have bad responses.

Looking to the definition of *"belief"* the Gk verb 'pisteuo' means to believe; to be persuaded of; to place confidence in; and to trust.

The word *'believe'* appears more frequently in the writings of the apostle John than any other New Testament writers. John 1:50 illustrates how Jesus used belief to confirm Nathaniel's accelerated confidence in Him that demanded no further proof. Matthew uses the verb ten times in Mark 10 and Luke 9, but John uses it ninety-nine times.

Sometimes it is used in the middle and passive voices signifying to *suffer oneself to be persuaded* as in the case of John the Baptist or Peter's visitation.

But it is the noun form of this word *belief* that is translated in the Greek "Pistis" or "faith" that we use from Romans 10:17 and 2 Thessalonians 2:13.

Its chief significance is a conviction respecting God, His word and the believers' relationship to Him, *"for without faith it is impossible to please Him."* Faith acts on the promise by appropriating its reality.

A contrast of Belief and Faith is where we distinguish the difference between them. Belief is mental and stagnant, faith is volitional and active. We may have belief without the will, but not faith. Belief is a realm of thought; Faith is a sphere of action. Belief can live in the study, but Faith must come out in the streets and confront the challenge or circumstance.

Faith substantiates belief by giving substance, life, reality, and activity to it. Faith puts belief into active service and connects possibilities with actualities. "If you can believe" Mark 9:23 says "... all things are possible."Faith is acting on what you believe, it is appropriation, and it counts every promise from God valid. Hebrews 11:6 says *"But without faith it is impossible to please Him, for he who comes to God **must** **believe** that He is, and that He is a rewarder of those who diligently seek Him."*

Hebrews 11:11 illustrates this point clearly, *"Because of faith also Sarah herself received physical power to conceive a child, even when she was long past the age for it, because **she considered [God]** Who had given her the promise to be **reliable** and **trustworthy** and **true** to His word."*

No trial can shake **faith that has a definite aim or a chief goal**; it survives the loss of anything when tested and still remains victorious. Hebrews 11:17-19 and 1 Kings 18:41-46 in the Amplified Bible clarifies this point.

*"By faith Abraham, when he was put to the test [while the testing of his faith was still in progress], had already brought Isaac for an offering; he who had gladly received and welcomed [God's] promises was ready to sacrifice his only son, Of whom it was said, Through Isaac shall your descendants be reckoned. **For he reasoned that God was able to raise***

[him] up even from among the dead. Indeed in the sense that Isaac was figuratively dead [potentially sacrificed], he did [actually] receive him back from the dead."

*"And Elijah said to Ahab, Go up, eat and drink, for there is the sound of abundance of rain. So Ahab went up to eat and to drink. And Elijah went up to the top of Carmel; and he bowed himself down upon the earth and put his face between his knees And said to his servant, Go up now, look toward the sea. And he went up and looked and said, **There is nothing. Elijah said, Go again seven times. And at the seventh time the servant said, A cloud as small as a man's hand is arising out of the sea.** And Elijah said, Go up, say to Ahab, Hitch your chariot and go down, lest the rain stop you. In a little while, the heavens were black with wind-swept clouds, and there was a great rain. And Ahab went to Jezreel. The hand of the Lord was on Elijah. He girded up his loins and ran before Ahab to the entrance of Jezreel [nearly twenty miles]."*

In Matthew 14:25-33 Peter began to sink because **he lost sight of his chief goal**, which was to "come to Jesus on the water". This was the object of his faith and the "substantive" point of reference that Jesus identified as a legal kingdom logic or pursuit, notice:

"Now in the fourth watch of the night Jesus went to them, walking on the sea. And when the disciples saw Him walking on the sea, they were troubled, saying, "It is a ghost!" And they cried out for fear. But immediately Jesus spoke to them, saying, "Be of good cheer! It is I; do not be afraid." And Peter answered Him and said, "Lord, **if it is You, command me to come to You** on the water."

So He said, "Come." And when Peter had come down out of the

boat, *he walked on the water to go to Jesus*. **But when he saw that the wind** *was* boisterous, **he was afraid**; and beginning to sink he cried out, saying, "Lord, save me!"

*And immediately Jesus stretched out His hand and caught him, and said to him, "O you of little faith, **why did you doubt?**"* And when they got into the boat, the wind ceased. Then those who were in the boat came and worshiped Him, saying, "Truly You are the Son of God."

Here we must understand that the object of faith requires a clearly defined point of reference in order to sustain the intense, passionate focus necessary to embrace its reality, or accomplishment. Peter like so many of us having little exercise in faith became distracted by his familiarity with his natural limitations and inabilities against the constant raging of the storm and *"beginning to sink he cried out."* This is why you must exercise your faith daily for development and familiarity to strengthen your confidence and trust through frequent association and involvement.

For this reason Paul states in 2 Corinthians 4:17-18 *"For our light, momentary affliction (this slight distress of the passing hour) is ever more and more abundantly preparing and producing and achieving for us an everlasting weight of glory [beyond all measure, excessively surpassing all comparisons and all calculations, a vast and transcendent glory and blessedness never to cease!], Since we consider and* **look not to the things that are seen** *but to the* **things that are unseen;** *for the **things that are visible are temporal** (brief and fleeting), but the things that are invisible are deathless and everlasting."*

Peter's focus was suppose to remain on Jesus (the object of his profession) if he was to accomplish his aim instead of focusing on the storm. Keep in mind what you focus on will determine or command which realm will manifest for you, which will ultimately determine if you will sink or stand. In the New King James Version Hebrews 10:24 says *"Let us hold fast the confession of our hope **without wavering**, for **He who promised is faithful.**"*

The Amplified says *"So **let us seize** and hold fast and retain **without wavering** the hope we cherish and confess and our acknowledgement of it, for **He Who promised is reliable** (sure) and faithful to His word."*

A close examination of Peter's experience or faith experiment reveals three primary points to this Faith principle. They are listed in this particular passage to help us understand both what is expected from us and the position Jesus takes regarding each of our faith pursuits.

First, *"Let us,"* indicates that we are responsible for holding fast and seizing the promise from God we confess or profess in spite of the odds or the appearance of adversity. The thing promised or the thing we decide to pursue and are driven, led or inspired to aim at houses all the "grace" we need to obtain it if it is from God. Here our faith initiates the work of grace.

Second, *"without wavering"* indicates that the correct posture and the appropriate method for the accomplishment and the fulfillment of Godly promises are vital to their manifestation. James 1:2-8 says regarding a request for godly wisdom, *"My brethren, count it all joy when you fall into various trials, knowing that the testing of your faith produces patience. But let patience have its perfect work, that you may be perfect and complete, lacking nothing. If any of you lacks wisdom, let* *him ask of God, who gives to all liberally and without reproach, and it will be given to him.* **But let him ask in faith, with no doubting, for he who doubts is like a wave of the sea driven and tossed by the wind. For let not that man suppose that he will receive anything from the Lord; he is a double-minded man,** *unstable in all his ways."*

Third, *"He who promised is faithful and reliable"*. This statement ensures us that two-thirds, or the main part, of the battle or spiritual endeavor has already been accomplished and finished. Our part is to know or understand what He says about a particular thing (His will regarding it), agree with what He says about it, and act on it staying constant at heart to trust his word in spite of the threat of an unfavorable outcome.

Remember, I stated earlier that after we are convinced that a promise is for us we must *believe* that God means all He says about it and agree to all its truth without discounting any aspects of it. So our active belief (mental persuasion) may both trigger and strengthen our faith.

Now that we've established the main points there are two other important points of emphasis that may help to shed light on how the Kingdom system works regarding or faith acquisitions and endeavors.

Fourth, "Peter answered Him and said, *"Lord, if it is You, command me to come to You on the water."* Here we must understand that it was Peter by his own decision who initiated this faith exchange which he was able to succeed in initially. Only after he allowed his lack of exercise and practice to overwhelm his chief desire did he begin to sink. The point is that since God has given to every man the measure of faith, He allows men to use their God-kind of faith to pursue precious promises that they might obtain a better tomorrow.

I stated in the section on vision "As children of God we are given the opportunity to **"Live an Expectation Driven Reality!"** But we must refuse to have *sight* without *vision!* Sight is the limited function of your lower nature; Vision is the eye of faith (spiritual sight) that gives it immediate substance to *God-appointed realities*. Without vision faith is blind and stagnant because it has no object to hope for or nothing particular to look forward to.

God-appointed realities are offspring's of prophecies, promises or merely words from God that when revealed to us birth desire or aspirations that cause us to hunger for their attainment or manifestation. This is "righteous hunger" the kind of hunger Jesus said it is a blessing to have. But as you acquire this hunger you must be swift to write it down (record it) and make it plain for your pursuit.

Fifth, "Beginning to sink he cried out, saying, "Lord, save me!" *And immediately Jesus stretched out His hand and caught him, and said to him, "O you of little faith, **why did you doubt?**"* This point exposes the fact that God does not interfere without your permission or request by petition. Although He stands by and sees all we are going through, His actions and inclusionary methods are governed by our response to and use of principles that are designed to govern our affairs.

Again, this is why *"God's people are destroyed for a lack of knowledge"*. He watches over his word to perform it, not the wrong interpretation and application of it.

Before I leave this issue let's have a moment of "real talk' not theology, not rhetoric, not assumption, nor religious or traditional defensive posturing. Real talk about *"Walking by faith, not by sight."*

How can a man walk by something other than sight unless he has something more tangible as sight to substitute for it? So then to walk as effective by faith as we do by sight we need something in our faith similar to sight as is our natural eyes. This is where vision comes in to play. If a man's faith has no vision he has blind faith. Although blind faith does not cancel a persons' existence in the spiritual realm, it does make it difficult for him to succeed in the exchanges from a spiritual reality.

It is my observation as a pastor that this is where a great deal of confusion exists in the Kingdom of God. Many Kingdom citizens have enough faith for entry into the Kingdom but lack productive vision-filled faith to accomplish spiritual things.

Case-in-point: Vision creates hope with an aim which selects the type of promises faith must draw from or aim at because "grace" has been allotted for the manifestation or fulfillment of God appointed realities initiated by faith. God appointed realities are **targets of faith** designed to consume the attention and focus of the new creature mentioned in 2 Corinthians 5:17 to replace our focus and consumption on worldliness.

In other words, we are to frame our world using the same methods and measures that our Father, God used to reframe the world. Since life in the earth realm consist of two realities the one we see and the one God says, every area of your life or every issue you face can be changed to align with what God said about it if you desire. Remember, your eyes see things as they are, but your faith sees things as they are suppose to be. We who have the God-kind of faith see things this way: "Call those things that are not as though they were."

Hebrews 11:3 says clearly *"By faith we understand that the **worlds were framed by the word of God**, so that the things which are seen were not made of things which are visible."* (NKJV)

The Amplified says *"By faith we understand that the worlds [during the successive ages] were framed (fashioned, put in order, and equipped for their intended purpose) by the word of God, so that what we see was not made out of things which are visible."*

Again, this is the primary reason God said to Joshua *"This Book of the Law shall not depart out of your mouth, but you shall meditate on it day and night, that you may observe and do according to all that is written in it. **For then you shall make your way prosperous, and then you shall deal wisely and have good success."***

Through out the many years of my life I've had to face many challenges that this principle use of faith has enable me to subdue, overcome, conquer, obtain, and be delivered from. Targeting my faith to deal with specific challenges has become a primary measure I use to also succeed in my endeavors.

To date, I have been delivered from severe skin rashes that were labeled incurable. In the mid-nineties I was diagnosed with cancer, but after being led by the Holy Spirit to isolate and do target meditation, I stand today totally cancer-free. I've been delivered from extreme money spending habits that kept my family in financial stress regardless of how much money I earned. I've been set free from the need of having people in my life who don't align with my purpose.

I've learned how to love and accept people as they are without needing them to conform to my expectations. Most of all I have learned how to use my faith in a way that conforms to, and corresponds with, who I am and the fulfillment of my God designed destiny.

As I prepare to close out this important part of our reconstruction project, you will see the continuation of this discussion under the next discipline titled "My confessions need restrictions." I've prepared several examples and passages to assist you in grasping the importance of assigning your faith to chief goals and definite aims so that you can finally become the new person God intends for you to be.

He has already given you the power to become a son of God, but you must work out your own salvation with reverential fear by committing to Christ like standards, attitudes, beliefs, and responses. In these passages notice the response of Jesus in each case where specific targets were placed before him.

Related passages and encouragements for edification

Habakkuk 2:4, Romans 1:17, Galatians 3:11and Hebrews 10:38 all distinguish Faith as the only lifestyle that kingdom citizens are licensed to live. In fact Romans 14:23 says that *"For whatever does not originate and proceed from faith is sin [whatever is done without a conviction of its approval by God is sinful]."*

"Behold the proud, His soul is not upright in him; But **the just shall live by his faith.**

Matthew 9:2

> "Then behold, they brought to Him a **paralytic lying on a bed**. *When Jesus saw their* **faith**, He said to the paralytic, "Son, be of good cheer; your sins are forgiven you.""

Matthew 9:22

> But Jesus turned around, and **when He saw her He said**, "Be of good cheer, daughter; your **faith** has made you well." And the woman was made well from that hour.

Matthew 9:29

> Then He touched their eyes, saying, **"According to your faith** let it be to you."

Matthew 15:28

> Then Jesus answered and said to her, **"O woman, great is your faith!** Let it be to you as you desire." **And her daughter** was healed from that very hour.

Mark 10:52

> Then Jesus said to him, "Go your way; your **faith** has made you well." And **immediately he received his sight** and followed Jesus on the road.

Romans 4:19

> And not being weak in **faith, he did not consider his own body,**

already dead (since he was about **a hundred years old**), and the deadness of **Sarah's womb**.

Romans 9:32

Why? Because they did not seek it by **faith**, but as it were, by the works of the law, for they stumbled at that stumbling stone.

Galatians 3:5

Therefore He who supplies the Spirit to you and works miracles among you, **does He do it by the works of the law, or by the hearing of faith? —**

Galatians 3:8

And **the Scripture, foreseeing that God** would justify the Gentiles by **faith**, preached the gospel to Abraham beforehand, saying, "In you all the nations shall be blessed."

Galatians 3:9

So then those who are of **faith** are blessed with believing Abraham.

Galatians 5:5

For we through the Spirit eagerly wait for the hope of righteousness by **faith**.

Ephesians 2:8

> For by grace you have been saved through **faith**, and that not of yourselves; it is the gift of God,

Ephesians 3:17

> that Christ may dwell in your hearts through **faith**; that you, being rooted and grounded in love,

Philippians 3:9

> and be found in Him, not having my own righteousness, which is from the law, but that which is through **faith** in Christ, the righteousness which is from God by **faith**;

1 Timothy 6:12

> Fight the good fight of **faith**, lay hold on eternal life, to which you were also called and have confessed the good confession in the presence of many witnesses.

Hebrews 4:2

> For indeed the gospel was preached to us as well as to them; but the word which they heard did not profit them, not being mixed with **faith** in those who heard it.

Hebrews 6:1

> *[The Peril of Not Progressing]* Therefore, leaving the discussion of the elementary principles of Christ, let us go on to perfection, not

laying again the foundation of repentance from dead works and of faith toward God,

Hebrews 6:12

that you do not become sluggish but imitate those who through **faith** and patience inherit the promises.

Hebrews 10:22

us draw near with a true heart in full assurance of **faith**, having our hearts sprinkled from an evil conscience and our bodies washed with pure water.)

Hebrews 12:2

Looking unto Jesus, the author and finisher of our **faith**, who for the joy that was set before Him endured the cross, despising the shame, and has sat down at the right hand of the throne of God.

Hebrews 13:7

[Concluding religious directions] Remember those who rule over you, who have spoken the word of God to you, whose **faith** follow, considering the outcome of their conduct.

1 Peter 1:5

Who are kept by the power of God through **faith** for salvation ready to be revealed in the last time?

1 John 5:4

> For whatever is born of God overcomes the world. And this is the victory that has overcome the world—our **faith**.

Jude 1:3

> *[Contend for the Faith]* Beloved, while I was very diligent to write to you concerning our common salvation, I found it necessary to write to you exhorting you to contend earnestly for the **faith** which was once for all delivered to the saints.

This ends part one of the two-book series:

Structure: The Master Key to KINGDOM SUCCESS
By Dr. Finace Bush

Look for book two, part two wherever books are sold or online at:

www.FBJM.org

or email:

F.BushPublishing@FBJM.org

Bibliography

Barklay, William. Bible Study Series Commentaries. 2010. (accessed 2010).

Dictionary.com. Dictionary.com. 2011. http://www.dictionary.com (accessed April 8, 2011).

Dictionary.com, LLC. http://www.dictionary.com (accessed April 8, 2011).